ENGAGING
with...

Atheists

understanding their world
sharing good news

David Robertson

D0532476

thegoodbook
COMPANY

Engaging with Atheists
© David Robertson/The Good Book Company, 2014

Published by:
The Good Book Company

Tel (UK): 0333 123 0880
Tel (US): 866 244 2165
Email (UK): info@thegoodbook.co.uk
Email (US): info@thegoodbook.com

Websites:
UK: www.thegoodbook.co.uk
North America: www.thegoodbook.com
Australia: www.thegoodbook.com.au
New Zealand: www.thegoodbook.co.nz

ISBN: 9781909919099
Design by André Parker
Printed in the UK

Also in this series:
- Engaging with Hindus
- Engaging with Muslims

Contents

Engaging with...

Preface

Christians have a wonderful message to tell the world. As the angel said at the birth of Jesus, it is "good news of great joy, *for all people*" (Luke 2 v 10). But sometimes we have been slow to take that message of forgiveness and new life to others.

Sometimes it's because we have become *distracted*. There are so many things that can push the need to tell others from it's central place in our calling as individuals and churches. We get wrapped up in our own church issues, problems and politics. Or we get sidetracked by the very real needs of our broken and hurting world, and expend our energies dealing with the symptoms rather than the cause.

Sometimes it's because we have lacked *conviction*. We look at people who seem relatively happy or settled in their own beliefs, and just don't think Jesus is for them.

Or perhaps we have just forgotten just how good the good news is, and how serious the consequences for those who enter eternity unforgiven.

But sometimes it has been *fear* that has held us back from sharing the good news about Jesus. When we meet people whose culture, background or beliefs are so different from ours, we can draw back from speaking about our own faith because we are afraid of saying the wrong thing, unintentionally offending them, or getting into an unhelpful argument that leads nowhere.

This little series of books is designed to help with this last issue. We want to encourage Christian believers and whole churches to focus on our primary task of sharing the good news with the whole world. Each title aims to equip you with the understanding you need, so that you can build meaningful friendships with others from different backgrounds, and share the good news in a relevant and clear way.

It is our prayer that this book will help you do that with a neighbour, friend or work colleague who has no belief in God, or who has abandoned belief in God entirely. We pray that the result would be "great joy" as they understand that Jesus is good news for them.

Tim Thornborough
Series Editor

Introduction

This is a book about engaging with atheists. What does that mean? Perhaps it is easier to say what it does not mean.

This is not a war cry, showing how we can combat and argue with the new and aggressive group that I call "the New Fundamentalist Atheists". Anyone who has engaged online, or face to face with them will know how pointless and usually fruitless that is.

Nor is it really for those of you who regularly meet with philosophy professors who are well-read, intellectual atheists in order to discuss the philosophical proofs for God, involving long strange words.

Nor is the purpose of this short book to provide you with a series of knock-out arguments that will enable you to walk off the debating battlefield victorious. Neither is it a "how to" manual which will result in all your friends, family and colleagues becoming Christians.

This is simply a book that hopes to encourage and equip you to engage in a winning and winsome way, with the increasing number of ordinary people you know and meet in modern Western culture who are influenced by a worldview that either does not believe in God—*atheist*—or which believes that, if he does exist, it is impossible to know anything about God—*agnostic*.

I am not an expert. I am a middle-aged minister in a church in a small Scottish city. I have been engaged in ministry for 27 years in both the country and in the city. As a working pastor in ordinary local churches, I see the crying need for evangelism. We need more Christians. Church growth, church planting, church renewal and church reformation all require, as well as produce, new believers.

But how do people become believers? Through hearing the word of God. But how can people hear if they don't come to church, read Christian books or listen to Christian media? We need to go to them. In the past, our strategy for outreach has centred on big rallies, tent meetings, open-air preaching and door-to-door visiting—all of which still have their place. But the bottom line is that the gospel is best gossiped by believers who have a passion and commitment to telling the good news to those in desperate need of it, and who belong to a local church where the Bible is central to its ministry and life.

I have been seeking to encourage this kind of evangelism for a number of years, and have practised it myself. I am encouraged by the fruits of this work. Breaking up the ground and sowing the seed requires patience, love and hard work, but it does eventually result in reaping the harvest.

After writing *The Dawkins Letters*—a book that replies very specifically to the arguments laid out in Richard Dawkins' book *The God Delusion*—many doors opened to me. I could not walk through them all and so we set up the Solas Centre for Public Christianity, which engages with, and trains people to engage with, the atheistic/agnostic secular people of our day. We are absolutely convinced that church-based persuasive evangelism is the need of the hour and that it is possible. This small book will, I hope, help equip you to engage in those who believe there is no God.

We begin by looking at who the atheists are; in chapter two we look at beliefs and practices of atheists; chapter three looks at how we engage personally; chapter four is the longest and looks at how we apply the gospel to the beliefs and practices described in chapter two; chapter five offers some guidance on using the Bible in engaging with atheists; chapter six makes some suggestions as to how the local church can engage; and chapter seven offers some concluding thoughts.

I was speaking at a conference a couple of years ago and a man came up to thank me. He was very kind; "You and Tim Keller are my favourite speakers," he said. "When I hear him, I thank the Lord that he is on our side. He is so brilliant. When I hear you, I think 'I could do that!'".

I took it as a great complement. I hope that after you have read this book, you will be able to say "I could do that", and that the Lord would take our weak and feeble efforts to serve him and use them for his glory in bringing many people to himself.

Understanding Atheists

Chapter One

Who are the atheists?

The visitor from Jackson, Tennessee, was beside himself: "I'm so excited, I met me a real life *a-thee-ist*. I ain't never met a real life atheist before." The note of delight and surprise was evident as two cultures clashed—the religious southern USA and godless Scotland.

It was pointed out to our visitor that 14% of the US—some 50 million people—now self-identify as atheists and that that number is increasing. Nonetheless, any budding US President would commit political suicide if they announced that they were an atheist.

Even in the United Kingdom, where politicians famously "don't do God", most atheists in the public arena are not proclaiming their atheism from the rooftops.

For some atheism is still a negative term. Which of course it is. *A-Theos* is just simply the Greek for "No God(s)". One of the reasons that atheism has a negative press is that there is still in some minds, the idea of godlessness being associated with all manner of evils—from communism to sexual immorality. But that idea is fading fast. Indeed the new atheists are desperate to show both that they have a robust morality, and that the reverse is true—it is really religion in all its forms that is immoral and evil.

Atheism—the real numbers

Statistics about religion and belief are notoriously difficult to both collect and interpret. Those who might label themselves as "atheists" remain relatively small, compared with the number who would say they have "no religion". Even those who do not think of themselves as being part of any religion will own up to having beliefs in other things than a personal god.

So in the United Kingdom, although around 50% of people would say they do not believe in God, many of them might also say that they *do* believe in guardian angels and many more will believe in some form of "spirituality". Similar levels of non-belief are found in France, Sweden, Belgium and the Netherlands.

At the other end of the scale, many of the former officially atheist countries of the Eastern European communist bloc remarkably show a very high level of belief in God—over 90% in Poland, Romania and Bulgaria, while the Southern European Catholic countries come in between.

In other parts of the world, belief in God remains the normal human position. Even in Communist China the number of theists is growing rapidly. Some argue that atheism has passed its sell-by date and predict a resurgence of religion, even in post-modern, post-secular Europe. Others believe that any religious resurgence is only the last dying throes of a backward humanity, as we progress towards a Scandinavian level of atheist nirvana.

This book does not attempt to deal with these sociological and demographic prophecies. The fact is that every reader will know and meet with many people who do not believe in God. Those of us who are Bible-believing Christians are then faced with a dilemma. How do we communicate the good news about the Son of God to those who do not even believe there is a God? How do we tell them what God has said when they do not believe there is a God to say anything?

Much of our religious language is incomprehensible to them. And we personally are an anomaly to them—believers in an age of unbelief; nice people who inexplicably follow a nasty religion; modern, intelligent people who still believe in fairies.

Let's begin by asking: who are the atheists? It is not as simple as it sounds. Atheists split into as many different denominations as Christians! The danger with labelling is that we push people into groups and forget that each human being is an individual made in the image of God, with a complex variety of reasons for being the way they are and thinking the way they think. Therefore the following labels are not intended as absolutes, but rather, as helpful guidelines to understanding.

1. Functional atheists

Many if not most people may not be *theoretical* atheists, but they are **functional** atheists. That is, they may say they believe in God or in some "higher power", but practically they live *as if* there were no God. They may use the language of belief, but their belief makes not one iota of difference to their daily lives.

Hugo Grotius (1583-1645), the Dutch Protestant lawyer, spoke of people living "*esti Deus non daretur*"—as if God did not exist. That is where most of Western culture is today. It is not just that governments are secular—they are opposed to the involvement of religion in public life—but that our whole culture is either antagonistic to, or apathetic about, the very concept of God.

Thus media, film, art, music, politics, history, commerce, industry and science are carried on as though there were no God. I would argue that, in a world without God, people are confused and disorientated and therefore immerse themselves in hedonism (the pleasures of the moment), power struggles and materialism. Modern shopping malls are our cathedrals; mammon has replaced God as the reason for our existence.

2. New Fundamentalist Atheists

When Richard Dawkins wrote *The God Delusion,* he did so not to convert theists, but rather, to give a populist intellectual justification for atheist belief, and encourage the vast number of functional atheists to come out of the closet and self-identify as atheists. He wanted them to move from a pragmatic functional atheism (we will live as if there were no God) to an explicit belief in atheism (there really is no God).

Why do we call this "new"? The old hard-core Western liberal atheism of people like Bertrand Russell, Antony

Flew, Sigmund Freud, and Jean-Paul Sartre had been so successful that it resulted in the pompous and premature pronouncement in the 1960s that "God is dead".

The trouble is that by the 21st century it is clear that God, or at least belief in God, is very much alive and not just in the Islamic world. Dawkins, a professor at Oxford University, was horrified that so many of his students were theists, and at what he perceived as the increasing "threat" from Islam and the continuation of Christianity, even in the bastions of Western liberal enlightenment thought. After I wrote a response to *The God Delusion*—*The Dawkins Letters*—I was amused to receive a letter from a couple of his top students who told me that they were Christians, "but don't tell the boss!".

So the "new" atheism was born. Dawkins, together with his fellow self-styled "four horsemen of the atheist apocalypse"—Sam Harris, Daniel Dennett and the late Christopher Hitchens—set out to "take on" and deliver the death blow to what they hoped were the last dying throes of religion. Less deferential towards the religious, the new atheists were happy to use mockery, ridicule and contempt as their weapons in the fight. At times it seemed they were driven more by emotion than intellect. Their motto seems to be "There is no God and I hate him"!

They give apocalyptic warnings about the end of the world being caused by the virus of religion, which needs to be eradicated. They hold conferences, rallies and never-ending debates on social media. My postbag is full of hate mail from people who get outraged at the slightest questioning of their prophets and beliefs. Some of the scariest groups are the American New Fundamentalist Atheists, who seem to be aping the worst of their religious fundamentalist counterparts. Arrogant, aggressive and intolerant, they use the internet widely to develop their own particular brand of "hate speech", all done in the name of "tolerance" and "clear-thinking". You will find that there is often a deep, emotional anger and bitterness in the NFAs—sometimes caused by bad experiences of religious abuse from the past.

Why do I call them fundamentalists? It is not just a rhetorical jibe (that would not be very Christian of me, would it?), but rather, because it is an accurate description. They have fundamental beliefs, which they are as emotionally committed to as any religious fundamentalist. Even to question these beliefs is to invite scorn, mockery and ridicule on a scale that is quite shocking to many Christians. And to many atheists also. It's why there has been a recent trend to a "nicer, softer" atheism, exemplified by writers such as Alain de Botton and the people behind the Atheist Church movement.

3. Agnostic Atheists

The New Fundamentalist Atheists are perhaps best described as *anti-theists* rather than a-theists. The vast majority of atheists are not like them, although it is still good for you to be prepared when they come your way. Most of the atheists you will meet are in reality *a-gnostics* (Greek for "no-knowledge"). It seems reasonable and humble to admit that we do not know; that we cannot know. The softer position says "I do not know because there is not sufficient information. I can't prove there is no God and you can't prove there is. Provide me with the information and of course I would believe."

This position is best summed up by Bertrand Russell's statement that if he met God and was asked why he did not believe, he would declare: "Because you did not provide enough evidence". Perhaps apathy is the predominant thought here. Many of your friends who fall into this general category do not lie on their beds at night pondering the meaning of life and suffering from existential angst. They are far more concerned about the game they have just watched, the bills they need to pay, and their next visit to the doctor. Normal life for them simply does not involve God in any way, shape or form.

4. Christian Atheists

Christian atheists? Is this the old joke of the man in the Belfast street, who, on pronouncing himself an atheist, was asked: "Yes but are you a Protestant atheist or a Catholic atheist?" This is an important category for us to think about because it recognises that religion is often cultural and tribal. I have regularly come across people who attend church but don't believe in God—ironically there are even some who make their living out of Christianity who don't believe in God.

But when we speak of Christian atheism, we are not talking about cultural Christianity or hypocrisy; we are reflecting on the observation that as regards all gods except Jesus Christ we are atheists. From the beginning, Christians, because they did not have temples, sacrifices and priests, *were accused of being atheists*—something which the early Christian leader Justin Martyr readily admitted:

And we confess that we are atheists, so far as gods of this sort are concerned, but not with respect to the most true God, the Father of righteousness and temperance and the other virtues, who is free from all impurity.

First Apology

Christians must be careful not to fall into the trap of, on the one hand, just applauding "faith" and "religion" in general, or on the other hand, coming across as the arrogant purveyors of one particular myth. The bottom line is that the Bible says a whole lot more against idolatry and the worship of *false* gods, than it does against atheism. Worshipping the wrong gods, or the right God in the wrong way, is just as reprehensible as refusing to worship God at all.

Reflection

- Think of some of the people you know—friends, neighbours, colleagues, perhaps even people at your church. What kind of atheism do you think they are practising?

- What influences in their lives do you think led them to this position?

- How might you have a gentle, friendly, non-confrontational conversation with them that explores the roots of their understanding? What questions might you ask them?

- Think about the influences that have shaped your own belief in God—family, life experiences, thought processes, etc. How might your atheist friends explain and understand your Christian faith?

Do try to understand why people become atheists.

Don't assume you do understand what they think and how they got there.

Do recognise that atheists come in many different shapes and sizes and cannot all be lumped together.

Don't place labels on people and forget their basic humanity.

Do ask if you live your life in such a way that your belief in God is self-evident.

Don't assume that everyone who lives differently is more ignorant or more "evil" than you.

Talking points

- If someone says they are an atheist, it's good to ask: *"Do you mean that you are 100% rock-solid certain that there is not and cannot be a God of any kind?"* Most often people will admit to some doubt, in which case, they might be better described as an agnostic.

- You might follow this question up by asking: *"What things make you wonder if there might be something or someone 'out there'?"* This can help to identify areas for a more fruitful conversation.

- Ask your friend to give an account of their "spiritual journey". What experiences led them to their current way of thinking? Who were the big influences on their thinking. What were the big negative things that pushed them away from belief in God?

- Why not ask: *"What would make you believe in God? What evidence would you look for?"*

Definitions

It's important to understand the difference between the various terms that atheists and others use to describe themselves. This list is not exhaustive:

Atheist/ism: Someone who does not believe in the existence of God.

Anti-theist/ism: Someone who strongly opposes religion or any belief in a deity. Only some atheists will be antitheists; for example, the New Fundamentalist Atheists described in this chapter..

Agnostic/ism: Someone who believes that claims about the existence or non-existence of any deity, as well as other religious claims, are unknown or unknowable.

Apa-theist/ism: also known as pragmatic atheism or practical atheism—is acting with apathy, disregard, or lack of interest towards belief or disbelief in a deity.

Humanist/Secular humanist/ism: the view that truth should be formed on the basis of logic, reason, and evidence, as opposed to what they consider to be 'irrational' religion. Historically not all humanists have been atheists, (the Reformers would have regarded themselves as Christian humanists) but the movement today would assume atheism as part of its philosophy. Humanism deals with humanity without God. Freethought/freethinker is another name some humanists adopt.

Secularist/ism: Those who believe in, and argue for, the removal of religious influence from public life. Secularists are not necessarily atheists, but in practice most are. More militant secularists tend to be atheists who are using secularism in order to attack religion.

Sceptic: (Spelled skeptic in the USA.) Someone who claims to have a questioning attitude, especially towards religious knowledge, facts or opinions. They are rarely skeptical about "scientific" claims which they regard as empirical

Chapter Two

Beliefs and practices

According to most atheists, this should be a short chapter. After all, atheism is not a religion and does not have religious beliefs or practices.

So it's simple. Atheists just believe there is no God (or that there is not enough evidence to sustain a rational belief in the existence of God), and that's that. There are no atheist principles, doctrines or practices. It's just simply *non-belief*. Which would suggest that every atheist book, radio show or blog would be rather dull—simply repeating the mantra "there is no God" a million times until everyone accepted it.

But of course that is not the case. In a world without God, there are still many questions that need answering: how do we define good and bad; what is the basis for morality; what is the meaning of our lives; how do we deal with suffering, etc? Everyone thinks about these questions at some level. So you don't have to speak with an atheist for very long to discover that there is a wide range of doctrines and beliefs to which most of them subscribe—even though they may hotly deny it! The list is intriguing:

What atheists believe about atheism and life

1. **Atheism is not a belief or faith.**
   There is no, or not enough, evidence for God.
2. **If God did exist then, if he is the God of the Bible, he is an ogre.**
3. **Atheism is the default position of humanity.**
4. **Atheism/Agnosticism** is the default position of intelligent, open minded and tolerant people.
5. **Atheism is the scientific position.**
6. **Atheism is based on reason.**
7. **Atheism sets people free.**
8. **Atheism is the "progressive" position for society.**
9. **Some atheists do bad things** but it is in spite of, rather than because of, their atheism.
10. **Human beings are fundamentally good.**
    Humans don't need a Saviour like Jesus.
11. **Sometimes life just sucks** and we just have to grin and bear it.
12. **We're on the road to nowhere.**

What atheists believe about Christianity

1. **Christianity is a belief that's equivalent to a fairy story.** It is based on faith, which is defined as belief without, or contrary to, the evidence.
2. **The Bible is a primitive book** written by illiter-

ate desert shepherds who reflect the horrendous morality of their barbaric culture.

3. **Christians only believe because of their parents or predominant culture.**
4. **Christians are intolerant** bigoted fanatics and a bit dumb.
5. **Christians and the church are anti-science.**
6. **Christianity is based on revelation, not reason.**
7. **Christians are trapped, repressed and need to be set free.**
8. **Christianity is the "regressive" position for society**, a return to the Dark Ages.
9. **Some Christians do good things** but it is in spite of, rather than because of, their Christianity. Religion in general and Christianity in particular is the root cause of all evil.
10. **Jesus is unnecessary.** He was a good guy (if he existed) but the church has corrupted him.
11. **Suffering proves that the God of the Bible does not exist.**
12. **The Christian belief in the afterlife is pie in the sky when you die,** and results in Christians wasting their lives and other people's on this earth.

You will see that these two lists are mirror opposites. Let's go through them in a little more detail.

1. Evidence and faith

Atheism is not a belief or faith whereas Christianity is the equivalent of believing in the Flying Spaghetti Monster (the FSM often pops up on many atheist websites).

They think that faith is a commitment to belief *contrary* to evidence and reason. Richard Dawkins makes it clear how much he despises the very idea of faith:

> Faith is one of the worlds great evils, comparable to the smallpox virus but harder to eradicate. Faith, being belief that isn't based on evidence, is the principal vice of any religion. [1]

Here Dawkins is just following in the line of the mockers who asked King David: "Where is your God?", or those in Athens who scoffed when they heard Paul speaking about the resurrection of the dead.

2. The Bible

It is a book full of contradictions and errors. Its history is bad and its science worse. Dawkins regularly got a round of applause at his "rallies" in the US when he read out the opening paragraph of chapter three of *The God Delusion*, which is a well-written rant against the God of the Old Testament—who he believes to be the most unpleasant character in all of literary history.

3. Why people believe

Feuerbach in the 19th century taught in his influential book *The Essence of Christianity* that Christianity was primarily a delusion, a self-creation by human beings who were looking for comfort but ended up being oppressed by their own invention. This is a very common narrative among atheists, especially of the more militant sort.

---

1 Cited in A. McGrath, *The Twilight of Atheism*, Rider (2004), p 95

4. Tolerance and intelligence

Atheists believe that they are intelligent, peaceful, gentle, kind people who are tolerant of everything except intolerance. The following quote is often repeated: "A militant Christian shoots an abortion doctor, a militant Islamist detonates a bomb, a militant atheist writes a book".

5. Science

Christianity is the enemy of science. From Copernicus and Galileo to Darwin and stem-cell research, it is clear that Christians are opposed to science. Science has provided us with cars, toasters, medicine and smart phones. Religion just hinders scientific research and development. Most scientists are not Christians. Those who are just compartmentalise their beliefs, and if they are any good as scientists, leave their faith in church rather than bring it to the lab.

6. Reason or revelation

Atheists like to think and reason for themselves. They are clear thinkers. They don't accept arguments from authority and most certainly not arguments from revelation.

7. Freedom or repression

Christianity is perceived as, at best, an infantile delusion that we need to be set free from. It inhibits science, sexuality and society. The standard atheist understanding of history is that humanity is inevitably progressing, but is being held back by religion. Charles Freeman, in his book *The Closing of the Western Mind* (2003), gives a typical modern atheistic viewpoint—the narrative of history as atheists perceive it. A long time ago in a land far away (actually Greece about 2,000 years ago) there lived a people who were enlightened and valued reason, philosophy and science. Sadly, into this world came the dark forces of Christianity, and so Europe entered a 1,000-year Dark Age. But then, thank Man, the Enlightenment came along and offered humanity freedom and progress. Since then we have been progressing, gradually removing the vestiges of Christianity, but we must remain vigilant lest the Dark Force takes over again. Speaking of repression, surely everyone knows by now that the church bolstered by the Bible has always supported slavery?

8. Society

Atheists think that Christians are out to impose our beliefs on them. "My atheism leaps to life when private belief becomes a public matter, when in the name of a personal mental pathology we organise a world for others." Religion really is a massive impediment to the evolutionary progress of humanity. "The fact that religion may have served some necessary function in the past does not preclude that it is now the greatest impediment to our building a global civilization." Atheists may point to how great secular countries such as Norway, Iceland, Australia, Canada, Sweden, Switzerland, Denmark, the Netherlands and the UK are, and then contrast them with countries like Iran and Iraq.

9. Good and evil

Don't you know that Hitler was a Catholic? That Stalin trained to be a priest? The *Guardian* newspaper in the

UK ran an opinion poll in 2007 in which the majority of people agreed that religion was a primary cause of evil. Atheists, we are told, don't fly planes into buildings. It is priests and nuns that abuse children. Religious people abuse children. And they do so either because of their religion or because their religion gives them a cloak and cover to be able to do so. Religious people are just after your money—whether it's American tele-evangelists screaming from the TV screen, or the local vicar waving a collecting can to raise funds for the church roof, they are all the same.

10. Jesus

Jesus, if he existed, was a cool guy. He said, or repeated, some good things. He was a rebel, an outlaw, the first hippy, a moral teacher. But he was not God and the early church did not believe he was God. This was made up later on. Other atheists will say that Jesus did not exist at all, but was just made up later on.

11. Suffering

This is the classic problem. If God is good then he will want to prevent suffering. If he is all-powerful he will be able to prevent suffering. Because suffering exists therefore, it is clear that the loving, omnipotent God of the Bible simply does not exist.

12. Heaven and hell

Heaven is a fairy story made up to comfort children, help humans to cope with fear of death and keep the poor in their place. Hell is the product of a sick mind whose only purpose is to frighten people into submitting to religious authorities. Heaven and hell are in effect the carrot-and-stick approach of religious institutions towards their followers.

Not every atheist will articulate all of these points. The kind and gentle people who inhabit the world of the Atheist Church, where they want all the nice bits of Christianity (without Christ) will not buy into every aspect. Hard-core atheists (the ones who make the noise and run the campaigns) will go along with Nietzsche's evaluation: "I call Christianity the one great curse, the one great intrinsic depravity ... I call it the one immortal blemish of mankind".

Most of your atheist friends, family, colleagues and neighbours will not be hard-core Nietzschians but many will have been influenced by these attitudes. Our television screens have been telling us for decades that religious people are either interfering hypocritical old busybodies (Dot Cotton in *Eastenders*, Harold Bishop in *Neighbours*), sex abusing priests, or young fanatics who are as likely to pull on a suicide vest as they are a prayer mantel. How can we overcome these prejudices and presuppositions? We will turn to this in the next chapter.

Reflection

- How many of these arguments have you heard other people using?

- Even if they don't say them out loud, do you agree that this is what most atheists will think deep down?

- Are you ever tempted to think any of these ways yourself?

Do listen to what your atheist friends think and believe. Ask questions.

Don't get immersed in the bitterness, anger and dirt of the atheist online campaigns.

Do try to read widely—in terms of history, theology and current affairs.

Don't despair if you are not a reader, or don't have enough time. Try podcasts or even ask your church to provide basic information on worldviews.

Do question everything. Think for yourself. All truth is God's truth, so we have nothing to fear in any conversation. There is a healthy scepticism that we should all be exercising towards truth claims of any kind.

Don't believe everything you read or are told. Charles Darwin probably did not convert on his deathbed, Hitler was not a Christian, and Christians did not believe that the world was flat!

Talking points

- In many conversations, the objections to Christian faith may come tumbling out in a jumbled heap. It's important to slow down the discussion, to take time to understand each thought properly.

- *"I can see you're very passionate about this, but I'd love to understand a bit more clearly what you are saying about that subject. Would you mind just explaining it to me in a bit more detail?"*

- With each objection, an immediate response will spring to your mind. But initially at least, try to avoid the temptation to bat back an argument or a put-down comment. Proper discussion, rather than entrenched debate, will only flourish when you have established a proper respect for each other, which requires listening and thoughtful questioning.

- *"I'd love to share some observations I have about that question, but I wonder if we could find a time and a place where we can focus properly on it?"*

- It is really important to show that you clearly understand the depth of the objection, and do not dismiss it. One way to do that it is to state it back to them, in its best possible form. Sometimes it helps to establish your credibility by going even further with the objection than they have!

- *"So let me get this straight. You're saying that the God of the Bible cannot exist because of all the suffering in the world. Not just earthquakes, disease and pain, but the countless injustices there are including slavery, poverty and the agonies of loneliness and broken relationships. Is that right?"*

Ivan's story

I was born in Iraq. I come from a mixed religious and cultural family—my dad is an Arab Muslim, but kind of a liberal Muslim, and my mum is Armenian, so she's culturally Christian. My dad had to flee Iraq because of the political problems with Saddam Hussein, so when I was a teenager I was sent to study on my own in Czechoslovakia. I lived there for eight years, and I embraced materialistic philosophy and became an atheist and a communist.

To me, religion was basically a waste of time. I had no respect for religion because I thought it was all made up of fantasies and myths: that people twisted things to suit their agendas and created systems of belief to manipulate weak and disillusioned people.

One day I got very angry and lost my temper with the woman I loved at that time, and the relationship ended—she just left me. And I just couldn't face that loss; I just couldn't deal with it. It uncovered my weakness, and I realised that all this inner strength that I believed in was nothing, was worthless. And I suddenly realised: "I am to be pitied like those people I pitied before".

I started reading the Bible, and later on I started to go to church. There was this *Christianity Explored* course, so I decided to go and join it. As I'm from the Middle East, I always have a suspicious mind. So I tried to ask questions to find out if the leaders would tell me the truth, or try to twist things or soften things up so I would think: "Actually it's not so bad". I discovered that they were just plainly explaining what the Bible was saying.

And also I started to realise who Jesus Christ really is. I had had all sorts of ideas about him before, but I started reading his words; I started hearing the stories he said, I started understanding what he did—and he blew me away. I thought: "This is the person I always wanted to be like in my life. I never thought there was anyone who can be like this!" I was totally blown away by his integrity, and the things he did and the things he said.

You can see a video of Ivan talking about his experience at **www.christianityexplored.org**

Engaging with Atheists

Chapter Three

Engaging personally

But in your hearts revere Christ as Lord. Always be prepared to give an answer to everyone who asks you to give the reason for the hope that you have. But do this with gentleness and respect.

1 Peter 3 v 15

While a few will engage with atheists in public debate and a few more on internet forums, the vast majority of us are much more likely to engage at a one-to-one level. We talk to work colleagues, friends and family. Sometimes you find yourself on a plane, bus or train and you get into a conversation that opens doors to discussing the good news. Most of us feel very inadequate in these situations—what can we do? What can we say?

In the next chapter we will look at how we apply the gospel to the twelve beliefs we identified in chapter two.

In this chapter we look at what we do. It is important to realize that winning the argument may make us feel good, but that our real aim is *to win the person*. Peter tells us that we will be asked and then we must answer—but we must do so with gentleness and respect. This does not mean that we are to be spineless and insipid, but it does at least imply the following.

1. Listen and learn

The first rule of communication is to listen. If your friend says he is an atheist, you do not jump in with a list of the five theistic proofs, assuming you know what they are! It's by listening that you discover where people are at. Is the person you are talking with a know-it-all steamroller bully whose only interest is to demonstrate his own superiority and your inadequacy? Are they someone who has been deeply damaged and religiously abused? Are they a hedonist whose only interest is how this will bring them pleasure? It may be helpful to ask some more general questions, like:

- *Have you always been an atheist?*
- *What happened that drove you to this conclusion?*
- *What are the moments when you are most dissatisfied with atheism as a way of understanding life?*

These are questions that you also might answer truthfully as a Christian. There is always the danger that your honest answers may be turned against you, but done with care, with the right person, connecting with someone on this very human level can open up areas of discussion that go beyond merely fencing with ideas.

2. Question and think

The questions you ask are crucial. We do not pose questions to accuse someone ("why are you such an idiot?"!), nor to waste time, but in order for you to understand what is being said, and to help the person you are speaking to think through what they are saying.

There are many key questions that we must learn to ask in a constructive non-judgmental way. For example, if someone tells me: "I don't believe in God", rather than immediately leap to defend the idea of God, I simply request: *"Tell me about this God you don't believe in"*.

Once they tell me that they don't believe in a God who lives in the sky, or who is cruel and vindictive, or... I then point out that I don't believe in that God either and ask permission to tell them about the God I *do* believe in.

American apologist Greg Koukl calls this the "Columbo tactic", after the TV detective played by Peter Falk. Columbo would seem to dither through an investigation, but then lead the murderer to incriminate themselves by asking sharp questions they were unable to answer. Koukl says:

> The key to the Columbo tactic is to go on the offensive in an inoffensive way by using carefully selected questions to productively advance the conversation. Simply put, never make a statement, at least at first, when a question will do the job.

Thinking is a crucial part of the process. As we question, we get information, we think, we process that information and that leads us on to more questions. And so we learn and communicate.

3. Read

Consume good-quality media: books, magazines, newspapers and the internet. And keep an eye out for films, TV programmes and radio shows that provide doors for you to walk through, or hooks to hang the truths of the gospel on. It's good to keep a written record of quotes, articles, films, songs, etc. that have impressed you.

Many atheists take pride in the fact that they will only base their views on empirical evidence—hard facts. And yet atheist dogma is filled with warped versions of reality and half truths that they routinely trot out as evidence for their rejection of God. In conversation, it really does help if you know your stuff and are able to evidence it.

For example, I have often been told that Einstein was an atheist, and then I read in a reputable source that the great man actually said:

> I'm not an atheist, and I don't think I could call myself a pantheist. We are in the position of a little child entering a huge library filled with books in many languages. The child knows someone must have written these books. It does not know how. The child dimly suspects a mysterious order in the arrangement of the books but doesn't know what it is. That, it seems to me, is the attitude of even the most intelligent being toward God. [2]

A warning here though. Be careful of quote mining. And be careful of reading more into the quote than it war-

---

2 Cited in Anthony Flew, *There is a God*, HarperOne (2007) p 99

rants. The above quote does not teach that Einstein was a Christian, and all the evidence is that he was not. It is also better that your quotes come from your own reading and your own experience.

4. Communicate

"Papa don't preach." Most people today are terrified/annoyed/angered by those who they perceive are preaching at them. Sometimes as a reaction to this, people will talk about communicating without words. Some Christians even cite what St Francis of Assisi is supposed to have said (but actually didn't): *"Preach the gospel always, and if necessary, use words"*. It's an attractive idea, but a moment's thought shows how ridiculous a statement it really is. How else does one communicate news except through words? Of course I know that people are suggesting that we must show Christ's love by our deeds, and who is going to disagree with the importance of that? But words are a vital and essential part of that love.

Talking, of course, can take many forms. As well as face-to-face conversation, there is the phone, letter writing, text, e-mail, twitter and internet forums. All of these can be useful provided they are used wisely and appropriately, but by far the best is the person-to-person, face-to-face conversation.

5. Begin where people are...

... and lead them to the logical conclusion of their beliefs. This is a crucial thing to understand. You start where people are and by asking questions and making comparisons, try to help them. Some people suggest that it is wrong to argue. But it depends on what you mean by arguing. Having a discussion which seeks to think, persuade and communicate, is not a bad thing. Helping people to think through their position, and understand it (and yours), can only be positive.

6. Love

There is a world of difference between producing a reasoned proof and persuading a person. Love means that you treat people in the way *you* want to be treated. Love, Christ's way, means that you are prepared to give and sacrifice, even for those who are your enemies. When people hate us—much as we would like to call down holy fire on those who abuse, mock and ignore us—we must return that hatred with love. That is never easy.

Love is also patient. We need to consider how we respond to abuse. On a personal one-to-one level it rarely comes to that (unless it is with close family!), but sometimes in the workplace or among friends receiving abuse can be quite uncomfortable. In my view we should stand up to what amounts to bullying, not for our own sake, but for the sake of others who may come after us.

Likewise on the internet and with social media. Richard Dawkins encouraged his followers at one of his rallies to: *"mock them, ridicule them"*. An instruction which some are all too happy to obey. But others in the committed atheist camp are embarrassed by this approach. For example, Ariene Sherine of the atheist bus campaign declared: *"the scathing slurs of my fellow atheists make me despair"*.

Love also means you don't fake it. You don't pretend. You don't engage in the Devil's favourite pastime of hypocrisy. And you must be incredibly honest. Resist the temptation to misrepresent atheist arguments or present the atheists' worst case. Instead, listen to what is being said and be faithful in responding to it. Don't twist words. Don't lie. Don't misrepresent. The Devil is the father of lies. The way of Christ is always to speak the truth in love.

7. Pray

It is important that you pray for those you are seeking to share the good news with. Nothing we can do or say on its own will ever persuade anyone. It is only as the Holy Spirit takes his word and our witness, and applies that to the hearts and minds of the recipients, that people are born again. This is a massive relief for us all. Yes, I will work at how I share the message of Christ clearly, intelligently and attractively. But the end result is not down to me. I have not failed if someone rejects the gospel. I simply continue to pray that the Lord will do his work of opening blind eyes to the glory of Jesus (see 2 Corinthians 4 v 6).

A friend called Richard, who had been an atheist at one point, was asked what caused him to change his mind. Was it the brilliance of the speaker? The atmosphere at the event? What he read? His answer was simple—"I think the Holy Spirit had something to do with it".

As well as praying *for* people, stories *about* prayer can be helpful as evidence for God in our conversations. Personal stories of answered prayer can of course be dismissed as untrue or as explicable in another way—but for many people they are at least part of the evidence they need that God is real, at work in the world, and concerned about the details of our lives.

It may also be worth offering to pray *for* someone. If someone shares a particular need, you might say: "Look, I know you have lots of doubts and questions about God, but I believe in a God who loves us, and who listens to our prayers for help. Would you mind if I prayed for you?" Even if your offer is dismissed, you have expressed your concern and love for them, and explained a little more about the God we love and serve.

8. Use the Bible

This seems so obvious that it need not be stated, and yet it is surprising how much we avoid actually doing it! The Scriptures are God's word to humanity. Faith comes by hearing, and hearing by the word of God (see Romans 10 v 17). We ourselves need to feed, meditate and drink from the word of God. But we also need to *use* the Bible. We don't have to cite chapter and verse, or open its pages and point to the words, but when we speak God's words to others, we can be sure that we are speaking the truth, and know that the Spirit loves to take the words he inspired and apply them to the hearts of those who hear.

There are those who think that theological study is as useful in evangelism as a chocolate teapot, but the reality is that without good theology you will never get good evangelism. The more we understand the depths and riches of the gospel we are seeking to share, the more we will be passionate, careful and insightful in the way we speak about it.

The word of God is a two-edged sword that cuts deeply into people's minds and consciences, but dare I suggest that we should never use it as a crude club to bludgeon people with? It does its own work. We are urged to make a plain statement of the truth, but we can do this with gentleness and respect. Here are some phrases we can use to add gentleness to our truth-telling:

- *"I was reading something in the Bible the other day that shed some light on this issue for me..."*
- *"It's interesting you say that—Jesus told a story about the very same thing. Can I tell you what he said—I think you'll be surprised!"*

We need the Bible ourselves but we should also encourage our atheist friends to *read* the Bible for themselves. I was approached by a young atheist student after a particularly lively event in a Brighton library. Here's how the conversation went:

"The Bible is rubbish, why do you believe it?"

   "Have you read it?"

"No, I don't need to. I know it's rubbish."

   "That's not very intelligent, is it? Surely you should read it and know something about it before you can make that kind of critique?"

"Fair point..."

I discussed various issues for a while with him and his friends, and then we parted on excellent terms. A month later I received an e-mail from my new friend, informing me that he had started reading the Bible. It was a King James version (AV), and he had begun at Genesis 1 and was working through the whole book. I groaned and asked him how he was getting on. His reply?

   "It's scaring me because it's beginning to make sense."

Another atheist who became a believer wrote to me: "It was the word of God, not the words of David Robertson, that changed my life". The Spirit uses the word. Encourage your friends to read the Bible for themselves—but perhaps you could guide them to particular books in the library of the Bible.

I have always found that Ecclesiastes, Mark, the Psalms, Proverbs and Luke are good openers. There are more suggestions in chapter five. And it should go without saying that you should be prepared to *give* your friend a good modern, accurate version of the word of God. The KJV is full of wonderful Jacobean language and poetry, but is probably not the first Bible you should give a biblically illiterate, postmodern atheist!

9. Leave it

Sometimes we are so excited to be in a gospel conversation with someone, we can feel we have to say everything in one go. It can lead to what evangelist John Chapman described as "vomiting the gospel over people". It may make you feel good to get it out, but it is usually counterproductive.

We need to recognise that a change in thinking and understanding brought about by the Spirit is usually a long-term affair—people need time to process things. It is usually far more productive to have a series of shorter, focused conversations with someone over time, than one massive discussion that tries to cover every single question or issue that they want to raise. Jesus wants us to be "fishers of men", and there must always be urgency in our evangelism, but anyone who has been fishing knows that it involves a lot of waiting...

So if you think you have made a single point well, don't feel bad about closing off the conversation there, especially if you are in regular contact with your friend. If another question is raised, you could say: *I'd love to talk about that with you, but can we make a date where we can meet for coffee/drinks/dinner so we can focus on it properly—I want to be sure I understand exactly what your question is.* There will be other opportunities to talk and share the gospel, and the seed you have carefully sown may germinate as God gives the growth.

But there may also come a point when you need to heed Jesus' command to "shake the dust off your feet". There are some conversations that are just not worth having, or are better ended quickly. Don't get dragged into interminable arguments that wander down endless bypaths and keep going round in circles. Much of what passes for debate on the internet falls into this category. It may be important for Christians to put a stake down in the ground on social media and other forums, but they are rarely productive.

There comes a point when you must leave in order to pursue more fruitful opportunities elsewhere. We must be careful not to expend too many of our precious resources—time, money, creativity, and concern—on those who disregard them, while neglecting those who may be more appreciative to receive them.

10. Together

Who is sufficient for these things? The notion of the lone evangelist or the lone witness is one that is profoundly unbiblical. We do everything in community. It is the community of the church that is the most powerful apologetic. They will know we are Christians by our love.

In the community of the church, people should see the reality of the gospel in action, the effect of the words. Whenever am invited to a church to do an outreach event for atheists, I ask the organisers, "if I come to your venue will I be able to say at the end: 'come to this church and you will meet Jesus?'"

You do not have to be an expert in everything, or even an expert in anything, because in the church of Jesus Christ you have a whole army of fellow warriors and workers in the cause of the Lord.

What is the purpose of engaging in conversation with atheists? Surely it is to introduce people to Jesus. And the great thing about the gospel is that you can start anywhere and still end up with Christ. All roads lead to Jesus, because he is the Lord of all.

In the next chapter we will look at how we can do that. But it is crucial that we recognise the importance of this.

Since the heart of God's revelation of himself is the figure of Jesus Christ, and since the heart of the Christian story of salvation is the career of Jesus Christ, Christian apologetics—like everything else in the Christian religion, from worship to mission, from prayer to almsgiving—rightly focuses on Jesus Christ. The heart of the Christian religion is personal relationship with Jesus Christ, and it is this to which apologists hope to point their neighbours. Whenever we can, therefore, we aim to focus on Jesus Christ: not on Christian metaphysics, or Christian morals, or Christian church membership—although each of these can help the case as Christ is truly known through them. [3]

3 John Stackhouse, *Humble Apologetics—Defending the Christian Faith Today*, Oxford UP (2002), p202

Reflection

- Think about some of the conversations you have had with atheist friends in the past. Have they got beyond argument into fruitful discussion?

- Look at the objections to God and the Christian faith outlined in Chapter 2 again. Can you think of some "Colombo" questions that might be appropriate to ask when someone raises them?

- Do you find it difficult to love those who mock the gospel, your faith and deny God? Spend some time praying that the Lord would give you the love for them that he has for you.

- What examples of God at work in your life—answers to prayer and providential guidance, for example—could you share with an atheist friend.

- How would your atheist friend respond to an invitation to your church? Would they meet hostility or get a warm welcome? Would they meet Jesus there?

Talking points

- When we love people, we are concerned for them. In regular conversation, people will often share problems and difficulties. Why not offer to pray for them?

- *"Look, I know you probably think this is rubbish, but I believe in a God who loves us, and is in control. Would you mind if I prayed for you at home?"*

- If people are resistant to opening the Bible, it can be effective to quote, or to retell, for example, Jesus parables in your own words. *Did you hear the one about...?*

- Ending conversations can sometimes be difficult, but try to give your friend a positive feeling. *"I've loved our conversation tonight, and you've given me a lot to think about. I hope you've enjoyed it too. How can we pick up on this again in the near future?"*

This chapter has been full of dos and don'ts which I will not repeat, but for good measure, here are a few extra.

Do   be real.

Don't just read Christian books.

Do   discuss questions, theology and the word of God with fellow believers.

Don't get frustrated.

Do   make sure you take time out and you learn to luxuriate in the goodness and mercy of God.

Don't give up.

Philip's story

Growing up in a non-Christian family with intellectually gifted but unbelieving parents, I used to think that belief in God and the supernatural had been discredited by the advance of science, and was incompatible with liberty. Religious faith seemed to me to involve the blind worship of a cosmic dictator, and the abandonment of reason in favour of "revelation". Why, in any case, should I take religion seriously, I thought, when the existence of evil and suffering clearly discredited the Christian claim that our world owed its existence to a benevolent Creator?

My scepticism and hostility towards Christianity, which developed in my teens under the influence of thinkers like Ayn Rand and Bertrand Russell, grew even stronger while I was at Oxford. Then, at the age of 24, I met my future wife, who turned out to be a Christian. Shocked by the discovery that this highly intelligent woman was "one of them", I determined to find out whether there was any good evidence for the existence of God and the truthfulness of Christianity, making it quite clear from the outset that I was not prepared to become a believer just to cement our relationship!

I started to read C. S. Lewis. I did so for three reasons. First, because he had himself been an atheist. Secondly, because I respected his intellect ... If he could have made the journey from atheism to Christianity, perhaps I was mistaken in thinking that you had to bury your brain in order to believe in God. Thirdly, you couldn't accuse C. S. Lewis of being glib or shallow about suffering. Having lost his mother at the age of 10, been unhappy at school, and then gone on to experience the horrors of trench warfare during the First World War, he was obviously only too aware of the problem of evil.

As I read Lewis's three most important books, *Mere Christianity*, *Miracles* and *The Problem of Pain*, I found myself not only following in the footsteps of a person who had wrestled with all the issues that were troubling me; I was also discovering intelligent and convincing answers to all my doubts.

You can read more about Philip's experience
at www.bethinking.org.

Chapter four

Engaging with the gospel

Do not conform to the pattern of this world, but be transformed by the renewing of your mind. Then you will be able to test and approve what God's will is—his good, pleasing and perfect will.

Romans 12 v 2

But a man is not really convinced of a philosophic theory when he finds that something proves it. He is only really convinced when he finds that everything proves it.　**G. K. Chesterton,** *Orthodoxy*

It is a terrible mistake to think that the gospel consists of a simple formula that people can memorise, recite and follow.

Those who do think this often end up repeating the same phrases as though they were magic incantations.

Conversations with atheists, or anyone else, then end up with rather awkward, convoluted attempts to try and get *"Jesus died for your sins"* into the discussion.

It is just as bad to pick a particular hobbyhorse and flog it to death. There are a distressing number of Christians who seem to think that the essential heart of the gospel is that the earth is 6,000 years old, or that same-sex marriage is the sign of the end times, or... The basic thing to remember is that the good news is all about Jesus—his birth, life, miracles, teaching, death, resurrection, ascension, pre-existence, church and word. He is the centre of the gospel revelation—from which everything then emanates. As C. S. Lewis argued, we believe in Christ as we believe in the sun; not because we see him, but because by him we see everything else.

Those who are biblically literate, Spirit-filled, mind-renewed Christ followers should not have any difficulty in engaging our atheist and agnostic friends with the gospel. We cannot convert and we cannot convince, but we can communicate. We are heralds of God's word, not pontificators about our particular beliefs, thoughts and cultures.

That's why it is essential that 1) we know what that word is and how it applies to our lives, and 2) are prepared and equipped to share what we have received. We find the common ground, and then we build upon that. Let's look at the twelve atheist beliefs of chapter two, in the light of what the good news says.

1. Evidence and Faith

Does the Bible ask us to have faith without evidence?

Is faith in and of itself a virtue? *No.*

It is what or who we have faith in that matters, not the fact of faith itself. The atheist tends to have faith in their own ability to judge any evidence that there may be. We live in a culture that tells us constantly we have to believe in ourselves—all this with very little evidence. But the Christian goes a different route. It is only when we believe in the Lord Jesus Christ that we are saved. It is not just that we believe something *about* God—it is that we commit our lives *to* him. And we believe because of the evidence we have.

We don't demand absolute proof—not least because we know that we are incapable of judging what absolute proof is—but we do pray for evidence. We ask to be able to see. It's not that we have visions or miracles every day—but we do take all the evidence we can, and on the basis of that commit ourselves to Jesus Christ.

Your atheist friend will ask you: *"What evidence?"* Be careful how you answer that question.

To someone who believes as an article of their faith that there can be no such evidence, anything you say will be discounted. It's like arguing with a conspiracy theorist—everything you say will automatically be dismissed as part of the conspiracy. On the other hand, there are more open-minded people who will genuinely consider what you have to say.

It's good for you to know not just *whom*, but *why* you have believed. In *The Dawkins Letters* I list the 10 main reasons for believing that I have found most compelling. Why not make your own list? And remember about asking questions—why not ask this simple question:

You want evidence—what evidence would you accept?

That is always an interesting conversation starter!

2. The Bible

When discussing the Bible, it is rare to find an atheist who has actually read it. In older people there are vague recollections of readings from school and church. In younger people there are various cultural references—usually negative ones.

This biblical illiteracy is seen even in those who are writing against the Bible. Dawkins justifies his own ignorance of theology by comparing it with his ignorance of "fairy-ology". This does not stop him making theological pronouncements, nor did it result in him writing *The Fairy Delusion*.

The atheist world is full of myths about the Bible that people believe to be true but have no evidence for. For example, Michael Onfray boldly tells his readers: "Genesis reports that God began from nothing" and that "Christians insist the world is 4,000 years old, no more no less". A great deal of what you have to do is clear away these kinds of misconceptions. Some Christians may *calculate* that the earth is 6,000 years old, but the Bible says nothing about the age of the earth. And the whole point about God is that he is eternal. He has no beginning.

It is astonishing that so many atheists waste time arguing about who created God—as though this were a major problem for believers. No Christian believes in a created God and you should not even begin to try and defend that idea. When even intelligent atheists such as Dawkins and Onfray make such major errors, it is little wonder that the more ordinary atheist just gets confused.

I suspect that the constant battering that the Bible has taken from public pronouncements has left many Christians unsure and uncertain, not least because many belong to churches where not only the trustworthiness but also the sufficiency of the Scriptures are called into question. We need to regain our confidence in the word of God, rather than the opinions of men. Abraham Lincoln is always a good person to quote:

> The Bible is the best gift God has ever given to men. All the good from the Saviour of the world is communicated through this book.

But what about the Old Testament God? Many atheists will trot out what they believe to be an obvious truth—that the God of the Old Testament is vengeful and wrathful, but that the message of Jesus is all about love. Miroslav Volf, the Croatian theologian, because of his experience of the Balkan wars, brings a different perspective. He makes this perceptive point:

> God isn't wrathful *in spite* of being love. God is wrathful *because* God is love.

When we see something we love being destroyed, when we see someone we love being harmed and ruined, of course we are angry with those who are doing it. The Old Testament message foretells the coming of the Lord in salvation, and the New Testament message foretells the coming of the Lord in judgment! There is not an OT God, and an NT God. There is one God—the God revealed to us in the whole Bible.

3. Why people believe

Again, I am somewhat surprised at how many otherwise intelligent atheists regard this as a killer point. *You only believe in Jesus because you were brought up in a Christian community. If you were brought up in Pakistan or Iran or China, you would have different beliefs.*

In other words, all beliefs are culturally conditioned. Of course if that is true, then it applies to the atheist belief system also—you are far more likely to be an atheist if, like Stephen Hawking, you were brought up in a Western liberal, middle-class, atheistic home. That even includes those who believe that their belief is not a belief! The conditioning is deep.

Swiss-British philosopher Alain de Botton is at least honest:

I was brought up by a father who made Richard Dawkins look open-minded on the matter of there perhaps being a supreme being ... I simply can't imagine joining a faith that is very foreign to me in terms of my background. I would feel it to be a betrayal of my family. By accepting the Father, I'd be going against my father.[4]

The other problem with this belief about faith is that I

---

4 Cited in *Christianity* magazine, April 2012.

have met many people who have been brought up in Pakistan, Iran and China who *are* Christians. An atheist journalist from *The Financial Times* came to do a piece on our small church in Dundee. After visiting the morning service, he came up to the manse for lunch with my family and several young members of the congregation. "Of course," he opined, "everyone here believes because of how they were brought up". I replied: "I don't know; why don't you ask them?" Much to his astonishment, every single person in the room had been brought up in a non-religious home. Kind of blew his theory apart. Sometimes experience has a way of doing that!

4. Tolerance and intelligence

This is one of my favourite myths—the myth of atheist tolerance. *A militant Christian shoots an abortion doctor; a militant Islamist detonates a bomb; a militant atheist writes a book.* In their own mythology, atheists are peaceful, gentle, kind people who are tolerant of everything except intolerance. It's a nice idea. What a shame it is completely false! What they do not see is that their striving for justice and equality is an echo of the Christian influence on our society. Before Christ, the world was a terrible place, as it still is in many places where his influence and teaching have not penetrated society:

> The pagan cult was never more tolerant than in its tolerance—without any qualms of conscience—of poverty, disease, starvation and homelessness, of gladiatorial spectacle, crucifixion, the exposure of unwanted infants or the public slaughter of war

captives, or criminals on festive occasions; of, indeed, almost every imaginable form of tyranny, justice, depravity or cruelty.[5]

The world before Christ was intolerant. And the world after Christ is just as intolerant. We need to point out that Christianity is the foundation of the modern idea of equality and tolerance. These things that we are enjoying are Christian fruits. But if the roots are removed, then the fruits will inevitably be lost in due course as well.

What about intelligence? We have to argue that Christianity is a rational, intelligent religion, in which we are encouraged to use our minds to their full, if limited, potential. The Bible is the key to opening our minds, not closing them.

5. Science

The idea that science and religion are in perpetual conflict is no longer taken seriously by any major historian of science, despite its popularity as an idea in the late 19th century. One of the last remaining bastions of atheism survives only at a popular level—namely the myth that atheistic, fact-based science is permanently at war with faith-based religion.

Yet this is one of the most persistent myths of atheist thought, and sadly one that some Christians have bought into. Again, there is way too much to deal with here, but it is essential that you have access to books that deal with this

---

5 David Berlinski, *Atheist Delusions—The Christian Revelation and its Fashionable Enemies*, Yale (2009), p 19.

issue. John Lennox's *God's Undertaker: Has science buried religion?* is a wonderful resource for thinking through how to answer this question. It demonstrates that not only are Christianity and modern science compatible, but that without the theistic worldview it is doubtful whether contemporary science would exist at all.

An Indian observer of our Western culture, Vishal Mangalwadi, is astonished that our culture is turning away from the very source of its science. "Britain gave universities to India to set us free. The West is now giving its youth myths that can only enslave them. This is ironic because it was the West's quest for truth that birthed science."

The trouble is that Dawkins and other atheistic scientists deliberately confuse science with the philosophy of *scientism*. The former examines the physical world; the latter is the philosophical (=religious) belief that the physical world is all that there is. Christians have a much bigger picture. We love science. We rejoice in science. We believe it is the examining of God's book of nature. But we also recognise its limits.

Many atheists speak as though science is omnipotent, and are very unwilling to recognise that there are many things that all rational people accept as true that cannot be proved by the scientific method. There is a lovely moment when Christian philosopher William Lane Craig takes on atheist Peter Atkins' challenge to identify some things that science cannot prove, but are true—he produces a devastating list that leaves Atkins speechless.[6]

The quantum physicist, Erwin Schrodinger, knew the

---

6 www.youtube.com/watch?v=3vnjNbe5lyE accessed 28.08.2014.

limits of science too:

> The scientific picture of the world around me is very deficient. It gives me a lot of factual information, puts all our experience in a magnificently consistent order, but it is ghastly silent about all and sundry that is really near to our heart, that really matters to us. It cannot tell us a word about the sensations of red and blue, bitter and sweet, physical pain and physical delight; it knows nothing of beautiful and ugly, good or bad, God and eternity. Science sometimes pretends to answer questions in these domains, but the answers are very often so silly that we are not inclined to take them seriously.

In terms of science itself, it does not prove God—because that depends on the presuppositions you bring to the table. However, science is not neutral. It is evidence that points towards God. It is part of the evidence that causes us to believe in God. For example, British astronomer Sir Fred Hoyle said that nothing shook his atheism more than the discovery of the fine-tuning of the universe, while the Big Bang is powerful confirmation of the Bible's statement that the universe had a beginning.

6. Reason or revelation

Atheists love to present themselves as driven purely by argument and evidence; and they then caricature Christians as those who believe in an "irrational" revelation from God. This is both false and unreasonable. If there is an almighty God who wishes to communicate with us, then why is it unreasonable to believe that he has in fact done so? The atheists set up this false choice—one that the Bible challenges. We are to search the Scriptures. We are to let our minds be renewed. It is the Eastern religions which demand that we empty our minds, not Christianity.

And although we believe that God has revealed himself to us supremely in the living Word—Jesus Christ—and through his written word—the Bible—we do not view his life or the Bible as opaque to rational investigation. We can present the Gospels for what they are—historical documents written close in time to the events they describe. We have ample, compelling and growing evidence of the historical reliability of the texts of the Gospels and the picture of Jesus they present to us. So we can urge sceptics to come to the Gospels with a high level of confidence, based on good evidence, that they are reading the actual words and deeds of Jesus.

7. Freedom or repression

Human beings have been offered freedom by those who wish them harm many times. It never works out. Take for example the notion of sexual "liberation". This was not something invented in California in the 1960s. The Marquis de Sade (1740-1814) wrote an infamous book entitled *Philosophy in the Bedroom*, in which he envisaged a 15-year-old nun escaping from the oppression of faith in God who "discovers all kinds of sexual delights, sodomy, incest and flagellation...". The link was clear: atheism made sexual experimentation legitimate and interesting.

But this narrative ignores the fact that the atheist version of sexual morality is itself incredibly repressive and harmful. Atheism finds it very difficult to have an absolute morality, and as a result morality, and especially sexual morality, is reduced to the dictum "as long as it does no harm". But who is to determine what harm is? If I sleep with someone else's wife, does that not do harm? Does sexual promiscuity not do harm?

After a debate on same-sex couples adopting (at that point, not long ago, same-sex marriage seemed unthinkable), my opponent and I were approached by several gay activists. During the course of the conversation, I was accused of repressing and abusing my children, who were then eight and six years old. Why? Because I did not allow them to experiment sexually! They proudly told me that if they were babysitting my children, then they would have no qualms in encouraging them to sexually explore their bodies.

To be fair my opponent in the debate was horrified by his "allies" and completely disowned them. But at least they were consistent. The paradox is that modern sexual "liberation" does not lead to freedom, but rather, to disease, distortion and destruction. By contrast, the Christian perspective is truly liberating. Again, we Christians need to reclaim God's gift of sex, and set it in the context of God's world and the purpose for which he gave it.

Every now and then you come across a secular columnist who is more prescient than many Christian commentators. For example, take this from Hephzibah Anderson, writing about how turning sex into mere biology has done so much damage.

In banishing religions from our intimate affairs over the past century, we've let science in, neutering and depersonalizing our passions by explaining them away as biological urges over which we have no real control. We have misplaced the human element of love.[7]

Our society has its own litmus tests of good and evil. Currently the most predominant is the attitude towards homosexuality and same-sex marriage. The perception of Christianity as homophobic, repressive and intolerant is one that does a great deal of damage, not least because there is an element of truth in it.

Of course there have been those who have misused their status as Christians, or who have warped Christian teaching in order to repress and suppress. But still we all agree that there are some things that *should* be repressed. Your urge to murder your neighbour as they blast out rave music at three in the morning needs to be repressed. Your desire to jump into bed with the beautiful young woman who works opposite you needs to be repressed—as does your desire to stuff your face with cream doughnuts whenever the opportunity arises.

You have to be very careful how you answer this objection. You have to listen to where it is coming from. And normally you have to go to the presuppositions behind the question before answering it. Avoid the twin dangers of using Christian jargon, which comes across as harsh and confusing, and of compromising the Bible so you end up saying the opposite of what God says.

---

7 Cited in *Prospect* magazine, April 2012.

But what about slavery? This gets mentioned all the time. Many Christians buy into the myth that the Bible supports slavery. It does not. No more than it does divorce. It *regulates* slavery in a fallen and broken world in just the same way as it *regulates* divorce. But the Christian gospel actually *destroys* slavery because it teaches that all men and women are created equally in the image of God, and that Christ comes to set the slave free. The historical and textual argument is complicated, but it is relatively easy to demonstrate that true Christianity frees and does not enslave.

The bottom line is that the reverse of what the current atheist worldview says is true. Rather than Christianity leading to repression and the hindering of "progress", it is true Christianity that liberates, and it is atheistic philosophy, with its false promises of freedom, that represses and destroys. It is vital to grasp that our "progressive" society is actually regressing into a Greco-Roman pagan worldview. Only Christianity provides the robust philosophical basis for freedom.

8. Society

Christians should freely admit that we want to influence society. More than that, we would argue that Christianity is a significant foundational basis of many democratic cultures—and we should ask what happens when the foundation is removed.

To say that men and women should not inject their "personal morality" into public policy debates is a practical absurdity; our law is by definition a codification of morality, much of it grounded in the Judeo-Christian tradition. [8]

We should reject the privatisation of Christianity, which would leave the church as the equivalent of a knitting club or Trekkie society. We are called by Jesus to be salt and light. We just simply point out that atheists do exactly the same—they talk of humanist and secular values as though they were universal and obvious. It is as easy to demonstrate that this is not the case as it is to deal with the myth of inevitable human progress. Most ordinary people know that we do not live in Disneyland, that it does not always turn out right in the end and that the world is not divided into the good guys and the bad guys.

Peter Hitchens (the Christian brother of the late Christopher), a former atheist, makes the astute remark that the worst place to be an atheist is in an atheist country; the best, in a Christian country. It is interesting that the countries most often cited as examples of secular tolerance and democracy are all countries with a strong Protestant background which has been strongly influential in shaping the culture and legal system. Is that coincidence?

It is also significant that the most authoritarian countries are largely Islamic or atheistic. The records of atheist countries like China and North Korea are hardly likely to appeal to modern Western liberals who have never operated outside a country with a Christian background.

Christian apologist Ravi Zacharias reports that the number one concern of people throughout the world

---

8 Barack Obama, *The Audacity of Hope*, p 218.

is *corruption*. Transparency International is a German non-government organisation that publishes each year a Global Corruption Perception Index. It is interesting that with the exception of Singapore, the top ten countries with the least perceived corruption are all Protestant secular countries. Mangalwadi observes:

> The CPI confirms what I saw in Holland—that the Bible is the only force known to history that has freed entire nations from corruption whilst simultaneously giving them political freedom.

Most people are not aware of just how much our society is built upon Christian foundations. The more intelligent and militant atheists do understand. And they are determined to remove the source of what they think is "the God virus". Our education, welfare, health and political systems are rooted and grounded in Christian principles. We should not hesitate to point that out.

The bottom line is that as Christians we need to argue that society is corrupt because we all, as human beings, are corrupt. And we agree with Tolstoy that the best way to change the heart of human society is to change the individual human heart.

9. Good and evil

It is not surprising that this particular myth, that religion is a primary cause of evil, has taken hold. Every week we hear about another "religious" bombing, suicide attack or beheading; we read of another priest abusing children; we hear the gossip about what is happening in a local church. It seems as though we are on to a real loser here. And yet it is precisely at this point that the truth of Christianity is demonstrated.

The worldview of most atheists is best summed up by the view that in the world there are good people and bad people. Good people do good things; bad people do bad things. For good people to do bad things it takes religion.

The trouble is that this view is way too simplistic. And it is easily proved false. One young atheist man asked me: "Why do you have such a negative view of human nature? I have to believe that human beings are basically good. Can you prove otherwise?" It wasn't difficult. We were in a bookshop so I told him to go to the history section and pull out any book, and I would demonstrate that humanity is messed up. Marek Edelman, the last leader of Jews persecuted by Nazi Germans in the Warsaw Ghetto to die, observed:

> Man is evil, by nature man is a beast. People have to be educated from childhood, from kindergarten, that there should be no hatred. [9]

There is no doubt that religion, like other powerful forces such as sex and money, can be misused.

> Does religious conviction provide a powerful reason for killing? Undeniably it often does. It also provides the sole compelling reason for refusing to kill, or for being merciful or for seeking peace: only

---

9 Cited in his obituary, *The Week*, 10th October 2009, p 55

the profoundest ignorance of history could prevent one from recognizing this. For the truth is that religion and irreligion are cultural variables, but killing is a human constant. [10]

And despite the protestations, atheist philosophy can also provide motivation for evil deeds. Lenin's destruction of churches, Mao's "Cultural Revolution", the 77 churches in Norway burnt by an extremist atheist group and Stalin's purges against the church all testify to that.

But wait! our atheist friends say. *That was nothing to do with atheism. Stalin's destruction of Christians was as relevant to his atheism as his having a moustache.* The amount of times this is repeated seems to indicate that some of the more fundamentalist atheists regard it as a brilliant point. It might be—if Stalin had burned down barber shops and locked up all barbers. But he didn't. Instead he attacked and destroyed churches because he hated them. He hated them because he perceived them as a virus and a threat. He regarded them as a virus and a threat because he was an atheist.

But what about the fact that he trained as a priest? He certainly attended a seminary until he was 14 but he did not become a priest. And even if he had, why would that matter? He changed. Aged 14, he read Darwin's *The Origin of Species* and promptly announced to his friends that they had been lied to, that there was no God. From that point on he lived as an atheist. To claim that this funda-

---

10 David Berlinski, *Atheist Delusions: The Christian Revelation and its Fashionable Enemies*, Yale (2009), p 19

mental change in his beliefs had no connection with his later actions is a claim that is based on wishful thinking and blind faith.

When we talk about good and evil, we talk about it in relation to humanity. This is really atheism's Achilles' heel. Although most atheists claim to be humanist, their philosophy, if consistently applied, would dehumanise humanity. As G. K. Chesterton pointed out—when we cease to believe in God, we cease to believe in humanity. On the other hand, the Christian doctrine of humanity is one of our greatest strengths. Christians know that everyone is valuable and valued, and to be respected and loved. We are the real humanists. Atheistic materialism really has no ultimate reason to distinguish between your neighbour and a dog, or a cockroach for that matter. Christianity does.

Bertrand Russell said that we are blobs of carbon floating from one meaningless existence to another. Richard Dawkins asserts at the start of his book *The Selfish Gene*: "The argument of this book is that we, and all other animals, are machines created by our genes". The Bible says that we are fearfully and wonderfully made, that we are all in the image of God.

At the end of his life, French philosopher Jean-Paul Sartre recognised that the Christian argument was more in tune with his own feelings than his atheist philosophy. His honesty about his instincts is an example to be encouraged in the atheists we converse with.

I do not feel that I am the product of chance, a speck of dust in the universe, but someone who

was expected, prepared, prefigured. In short, a being whom only a Creator could put here; and this
idea of a creating hand refers to God.

10. Jesus

All our evangelism is pointless if we do not point to
Christ. People cannot accept him if they do not know
who he is. It is essential that you have a good grasp of the
basic historical, biblical and theological teaching about
who Jesus is. It was for that reason that I wrote *Magnificent Obsession*. Get a book like it so that you have a good
understanding of the issues and so that you have a book
to pass on. There is so much misinformation and mythology around the person and work of Jesus that it is essential that you know the facts about him. What is even
more vital is that you actually know him. An old Puritan
prayer expresses this idea rather well:

> By reason I see a thing is so;
> by faith I know it as it is.
> I have seen thee by reason and not been amazed,
> I have seen thee as thou art in thy Son and have
> been ravished to behold thee.

Many people particularly have been impressed by the
evidence around the resurrection. Atheist philosopher
Anthony Flew, after his remarkable conversion to theism
late in life said: "Today I would say the claim concerning
the resurrection is more impressive than any of the religious competition".

11. Suffering

How can this problem be answered? Not tritely. Not with superficial and shallow sound bites. First, you need to find out if the person asking is making a plea (*Why, O God?*), or an accusation (*If I was God I would have done a far better job*). I suspect that most of us don't have the time to read the mountains of material written on this whole problem, although I would strongly recommend Augustine, William Lane Craig and C. S. Lewis. The latter's *The Problem of Pain* deals with the philosophical question, while *A Grief Observed* deals with the emotional ones. There is really no simplistic solution to this. Instead we ourselves must wrestle and know what the Bible says.

As a preacher I find it interesting that the series of sermons I preached which seems to have had most impact on non-Christians is a series on the book of Job. Why? Because the questions in Job are the questions that many people face—and the answers cannot be reduced to a formula. Sometimes you find that it is only when you have suffered yourself, as Job did, that you are able to comfort those with the comfort you yourself have received.

It is also worth noting that the problem of suffering is as big, if not bigger, for atheists. How can you deal with and survive suffering when it has no purpose and meaning at all?

12. Heaven and hell

The key here, as with all the other subjects, is to broaden the question so that we can understand the context in which it is asked. You don't immediately start discussing hell until you set the groundwork by discussing the whole idea of what happens to us when we die.

The atheist view is starkly put by Bertrand Russell:

No fire, no heroism, no intensity of thought or feeling, can preserve a life beyond the grave ... all the
labours of the ages, all the devotion, all the inspi-
ration, all the noonday brightness of human geni-
us, are destined to extinction in the vast death of
the solar system; and the whole temple of man's
achievement must inevitably be buried beneath
the debris of a universe in ruins.

Woody Allen expressed the more common fear of
most people: "I'm not afraid of death, I just don't want
to be there when it happens ... Life is full of loneliness,
and misery, and suffering and unhappiness, and its all
over much too quickly." The Christian view of heaven
is so much more glorious than that. It is not "pie in the
sky when you die" but more "steak on your plate while
you wait". If you can convey something of that glorious
hope, then you will make people "hungry for heaven".

But what about hell? I usually end up fulfilling God-
win's law (which states that the longer an internet discussion goes on, the more likely it is that someone will make
a comparison with Hitler and the Nazis), so here goes!

In the film *Downfall*, Adolf Hitler states just before he
commits suicide: "I will die and then I will be at peace".
Is that the case? Can we commit the most horrendous
crimes in this life and then be at peace in the next? The
biblical idea of justice, and a day of judgment, is one that
instinctively most human beings accept and warm to.
That is the best starting point. Any discussion should all

be kept within the parameters of the justice and goodness of God. We are not in a position to judge but he is. It is also worth pointing out that no one need go to hell. Christ has opened up a means of escape, and we would do well to point people to him.

Other fruitful areas

Many of the above subjects will be raised by atheists you are in conversation with, who will view them as powerful arguments against God. But in addition to these, I would like to suggest the following as great conversation starters which lead to the good news.

1. Beauty

It's hard to hold a baby in your arms, take a walk in the Scottish highlands, or listen to Bach—and be an atheist! One atheist told me that his atheism was challenged more by Bach than by anything else. Music and art become powerful apologetics for the gospel. Where are the great atheists' oratorios? The great atheist works of art? This is not to say that atheists cannot produce good art and music; it is to say that even such art and goodness points to the One Great Artist, the Ultimate Musician, in whose image they are made.

> Denying the reality of a spiritual core as the essence of every human being makes it hard to make sense of music, because music, like morality, is a matter of the soul. Those who think that the universe is only material substance and the soul is an illusion find it hard to explain music.

As I write this, I am sitting in my parents' home in the Scottish highlands, overlooking the Dornoch Firth. It is such a stunningly beautiful scene, as the sun sets behind the mountains to the west, the effect made even more peaceful and stunning by a gorgeous clarinet concerto being played on *Classic FM*. It is at times like this that I just want to turn to my atheist friends and say: *Really? You believe all this is just an accident of chemistry?* Beauty always points to the Beautiful One.

2. Community

Why has the atheist church movement begun? Because human beings are inherently social animals who have a longing for community. Most modern people have a sense that there must be something more than work, money, 42-inch plasma TVs, overseas holidays and 15 minutes of fame on the internet. People long for family and they long for community. The church of Jesus Christ is a great example of that.

I met A for coffee one day. He said: "David, I hate everything that you teach but I want everything that you have—at least for my family. In your church my children can meet people from different ages, social groups and races. They are treated with respect and love. Can you not have that without Christ?" To which the answer is "no". It is Christ who breaks down the dividing walls of partition. It is in Christ alone that our hope is found. I note in passing that the atheist church movement has only been going for a couple of years and already it has fallen prey to the all-too-human faults of in-fighting and splits. Without Christ, community is difficult, if not impossible.

3. Family

The atheist view of morality invariably destroys the family. The Christian view of the family is actually the predominant and moulding influence of our society's current understanding. We need to demonstrate to people that we are concerned with their whole families and the complex relationships that come out of family. Our concept of family works only when we realise that it is derived from the triune God.

4. Equality and social justice

The atheist world talks about helping the poor. Christianity just does. Money and how we provide for our families is something of vital significance to all of us. The old Italian proverb is correct: "He who leaves God out of his reckoning does not know how to count". We must be careful not to equate Christianity with any particular economic system, nor should we fall into the trap of espousing the health-and-wealth gospel, but it is right for us to point out that when an economy is governed on Christian principles, it makes a vast difference.

There is a reason that the Netherlands with its limited size and resources is so prosperous, whereas India with its vast size and resources has struggled so much. Two different religions and philosophies have predominated. As our society has turned away from God, we have instead turned towards the worship of wealth and prosperity. The atheist John Gray makes the brilliant point that "the free market became a religion only when its basis in religion was denied".

Do make use of the many resources we have available.

Don't think that because you have read one book, or heard one talk, on any given subject that you are then an expert on it.

Do try and get an understanding of the culture you live and move in. It's good to read a local magazine or newspaper and be aware of the kind of media that people are listening to or watching.

Don't get stuck in the 21st century. It is always good to get some historical context. Older Christian books, good historical biographies and secular histories are good ways to get a wider perspective. There really is nothing new under the sun.

Do always ask: "What does Jesus think about this? How does this connect with Christ?" He must always be at the centre and you must look for his light to shine on and in every situation.

Don't despair. You are not expected to know everything or have the answer for everything. The good thing is that you know the One who does.

Chapter five

Engaging with the Bible

The unfolding of your words gives light;
it gives understanding to the simple.

Psalm 119 v 130

One of our key principles is that we want to give people the word of God—that means the Bible.

I like to challenge some of my atheist/agnostic friends as to what kind of agnostic they are. I point out that there is intelligent agnosticism and that there is dumb agnosticism. In order to explain the difference, I ask them to imagine that I am sitting in my living room, watching Barcelona *vs.* Real Madrid in the European Cup Final.

The doorbell rings and it's a complete stranger who asks me: "Do you know your house is on fire?". I reply that I don't know. I am agnostic about it. A dumb agnostic in that situation says: "I don't know and I don't care". An intelligent agnostic says: "I don't know, but it's a pretty big deal if my house burns down, especially with me in it, so even though I don't know you, and I am more than a little suspicious of you, I will go and investigate". Likewise, you can encourage your atheist/agnostic friends to investigate. Perhaps by reading a book you give them, perhaps by going to something like *Christianity Explored* or *Alpha*, or perhaps by simply going to church with you.

But one of the best things to do is one-to-one personal Bible study. Why not ask your friend to read a particular passage and then meet them for a drink and discussion? Or perhaps even better, why don't a group of you—Christians and non-Christians—meet for open discussion on the issues raised?

Here are some suggested passages that I have found especially useful in opening up the issues that trouble atheists and agnostics.

Ecclesiastes

This may seem a little unusual but I have found this to be one of the best books to start people with. Why? Because it is perfect for postmoderns who are searching for meaning and just "can't get no satisfaction".

I remember a drug addict, P, who started coming to church. I gave her Ecclesiastes to read, and she came back the following week with a great summary: *"Man, that was totally amazing. I didna ken that all that was in the Bible—it's like Kurt Cobain on speed!"* I would suggest you get a good commentary (and listen to a helpful series of sermons on the book) so that you get a firm grasp of it. I love T. M. Moore's *Ecclesiastes: Ancient Wisdom When All Else Fails*. Then just simply do one chapter of Ecclesiastes at a time together. Always ask about the passage: What is it saying? What did Solomon find meaningless? What hope is offered or what hope can you think of? What would make this meaningful?

Selected Psalms

I always love to introduce the Psalms as the songbook Jesus knew and used. They are wonderfully contemporary, mingling human emotion and biblical theology in poetic form, bringing some of the great questions we all face to the surface.

Psalm 8: What is humanity?

G. K. Chesterton observed that once we lose belief in God, we also lose belief in man. It may seem strange but sometimes the way to get to God is through humanity. We are made in the image of God. If we understand who we are, we then get some grasp of who God is. Psalm 8 covers this, as well as the relationship of humanity to the creation, praise and, of course, it is cited in the New Testament as being about the humanity of Christ. Environmentalism, true humanism, angels and who is Christ—all in this one small song!

Psalm 14

This may seem a strange and somewhat "in your face" psalm to begin with, as its opening line states: "The fool says in his heart, 'there is no God'"! But it puts the question of atheism on the table, and shows that the Bible is not ignorant of the possibility, and addresses it. It is important that you understand that "fool" here does not mean intellectually stupid, but rather, morally culpable.

You should note that atheism is something that is primarily in the heart (the Hebrew term not just for emotions but for the inner being). Although there are people who have genuine intellectual questions, most atheists are not atheists because of intellect, but rather, because of emotion. Sometimes this can be demonstrated in spectacular fashion. For instance, the president of an atheist society was so infuriated at the end of being pressed on where his beliefs led him that he blurted out: "I don't care if you could prove God to me; I wouldn't worship him"! He thereby demonstrated that the main problem for many atheists is not intellectual but emotional and spiritual. They don't believe in God because they don't want to believe in God, not because the force of evidence overwhelms them.

Psalm 19

This looks at creation and the word. It is a great jumping-off point for talking about God's two books of revelation—nature and Scripture.

Psalm 22

Here we see Jesus on the cross. Why did Jesus feel forsaken? What did he suffer? Why did he suffer? What are the fruits of Christ's work? This is also a useful psalm for thinking about the problem of suffering, and seeing that a big part of the answer is understanding the meaning and reason for the suffering of the Son of God.

Psalm 51

This deals with issues of sin and forgiveness. Tell the story of David and Bathsheba and of Nathan the prophet (the context in which this psalm was written—see 2 Samuel 11 – 12). Why did David need to be forgiven? What had he done wrong? Why did he do wrong (born sinful from the womb)? How could he be cleansed? How can we be cleansed? What does God want from us? What can we expect from him?

Once someone recognises the need for forgiveness, the gospel is really good news!

Psalm 91

This is a beautiful song that deals with fear—especially the fear of ill health and death. It can also be used to explain the work of Christ and the place of prayer. And this psalm illustrates an important point in engaging with atheists. I think it is vital to use personal testimony in explaining how Scripture works.

This psalm is very precious to me because in 2011 I was in a coma and almost died. I experienced the "terror of night," and as I came out of that coma, I was in a difficult, lonely and frightening place. Psalm 91 (especially the beautiful sung version by the Australian band *Sons of Korah*) was a lifeline to me. Through that psalm God ministered to my heart and, along with other psalms, it was greatly used in my healing.

Sometimes it is not enough to tell people the facts about something as though it were just cold and clinical. Sometimes personal testimony can be very powerful; none more so than when the power of the word of

God is demonstrated. So tell your own story; share what for you is a precious part of Scripture that the Lord has encouraged, challenged or comforted you with at some important stage of your life. It may also be appropriate to give them a good book of testimonies to read.

Psalm 119

This is a song that explains the different purposes and uses of the word of God. The whole concept of revelation is an alien one to most atheists—although there is no obvious reason why God should not reveal himself. Atheists who complain about the lack of evidence that God provides can be shown that God's word is light, treasure, law, knowledge, true, trustworthy, eternal, delightful, boundless, wonderful, life and pure gold.

Psalm 130

A song for the depressed and discouraged. A song for those who are aware of their own sin and the need for forgiveness. A song that encourages patience and brings hope. Everyone needs redemption. Redemption songs such as this teach us about it.

Psalm 139

This is about God's knowledge of us and how we can know him through his thoughts. This song enables us to think about both who God is and who we are. It teaches us to recognise our mortality and number our days. Like all the psalms it is a prayer, and the last two verses are a great prayer to offer to someone who is seeking.

Proverbs 8

This focuses on Christ, creation and wisdom. There is a presupposition in much atheist philosophy that the "religious" are faith-based, emotional and irrational people. This chapter shows us the real source of wisdom and knowledge. Perhaps reading this in conjunction with John 1 and the first two chapters of Colossians would be helpful.

The Gospel of Luke

We are to tell people the story of Christ. Luke's Gospel knocks on the head from the very beginning the idea that it is just about myth. It is a very accessible book for modern Western (and Eastern and Southern) people. Asking someone to read a chapter of Luke per week and meeting with them to discuss that chapter—even for 30 minutes—is so worthwhile.

The Gospel of Mark

The *Christianity Explored* course is based on this, the shortest Gospel. I would suggest using *CE* on a one-to-one basis, complete with the DVD.

Acts

This is really Luke part two, and continues the story of the work of Christ. Acts was written in a different cultural context to ours and yet there is much that is similar. Looking especially at Acts 16 – 30, where the gospel comes to Europe, can be very profitable.

The fact that the gospel of Jesus is real history that took place in real space and real time is one that most atheists (and many Christians) need to grasp. Again, I have found that John Dickson's *Life of Christ* book and video series is an eye-opener and a real mind-changer for many people. It helps cement in people's minds that we are not dealing with Hobbit land or Narnia.

Colossians

Colossians is the letter for atheists! Or at least you can read and discuss it as that. It was written to a church which had to deal with false philosophies and religions. It does not present us with just another philosophy, but rather, with Christ as the antidote to all human philosophies. It also allows you to discuss some of the practical implications of Christian teaching—not least in the areas of family, work (and slavery) and church.

1 John

Sin, life, love and how we know God are all key themes in this wonderful and sometimes complex letter. The fact that a book of the Bible contains difficult themes and things that are "hard to understand" should not deter us from looking at it with non-believers. Indeed, sometimes the fact that we as Christians find parts of the Bible difficult, and that we don't know it all, is an attractive thing to non-Christians. We are not know-it-alls. We too are seeking after the truth.

Do read the Bible for yourself. Let it be your daily meat, milk and bread.

Don't assume that those you study the Bible with will have a knowledge of biblical background. And don't assume they are ignorant. It's important to have the context of both the biblical text and the contemporary culture.

Do take time to share, read, question and discuss with your friends.

Don't ever be arrogant enough to think that you have got it—that you understand all there is to know about the Bible. You will always be learning. Humble learning is a whole lot better than an arrogant know-it-all attitude.

Do be a doer as well as a hearer of the word.

Caroline's story

I believed in God as a child, but when I left school I met people who didn't believe in God, but appeared to be "moral", for no reason that I could fathom. I concluded that I didn't need to bother with belief in God, and I decided to live life on the basis that God didn't exist. From there began my journey downhill—spiritually, emotionally and morally—until seven years later I admitted defeat. On the outside, I might have seemed to have a lot going for me, but internally, I was plagued with questions:

- *I seemed to find more suffering than joy in life—so why should I bother to keep going?* At several points I felt strongly that life just wasn't worth it.
- *What hope is there for me if there is nothing after*

death? The thought of turning into nothing was deeply depressing and frightening to me. It was just a vision of blackness.

- *What meaning does my life have at all?* I am going to be forgotten soon. What difference would it make that I had been here?

- *How can anything in the world have meaning if there is nothing outside it to refer to?* It simply can't.

- *So what value is there in achievement?* Whose opinion is worth anything? My instinct was to want my father's good opinion more than anyone else's, but one day he would die and I would have no one to live for.

- *What need is there for me in the world?* I decided that people created a sort of interim need for themselves, for example, by getting married and being needed by that person. But it was a manufactured, not an absolute, need.

- *What is my purpose in life?* I had no direction. I tried to lose myself in music and the arts.

At the same time my conscience plagued me, since I was never as good or as good at anything as I felt I should be, and I found no relief.

In my second year at university, I asked friends about the purpose and meaning of life, but got no satisfying answers. During my three years at Cambridge I am not aware of ever having been approached by Christians with the gospel, even though I am sure that if someone had come knocking on my door I would have been open. So it wasn't until I was 24 that I decided I had to find out whether God existed, and a friend who had become a Christian set me on the right track. Then life began...

Chapter six

How can a church engage?

Engaging with atheists is not easy. It is emotionally, physically, mentally and spiritually draining. Especially the latter. You don't need to be the type of person who sees demons hiding behind every tree to understand that this is primarily a spiritual battle.

> For our struggle is not against flesh and blood, but against the rulers, against the authorities, against the powers of this dark world and against the spiritual forces of evil in the heavenly realms.
>
> *Ephesians 6 v 12*

You will note that the atheists are not your enemy. They are amazing human beings made in the image of God. They *are* enemies of God, as you once were. But it was while we were still his enemies that Christ died for us.

Our true enemy is far more serious and far more sinister. He is Satan, the accuser, the father of lies, the prince of darkness. He and his demonic forces are the greatest enemy we could ever face. That is why we have to put on the full armour of God.

There have been times in my own life when, after taking part in a debate, or an extended online conversation, or spending hours listening to an atheist attacking my faith, the clouds gather and the darkness overwhelms. C. S. Lewis knew this experience very well, as he wrote in a letter to a friend: "Apologetic work is so dangerous to one's own faith. A doctrine never seems dimmer to me than when I have just successfully defended it."

Fools rush in where angels fear to tread—and many of us just do not want to go there. And yet the love of Christ compels us. *So what can we do?*

We are not alone

The answer is so obvious that sometimes we miss it. We are not meant to fight on our own. We are to put on the full armour of God and we are to work together with the rest of the body of Christ if we are serious about communicating the good news. If you want to engage with atheists, you had better be prepared, equipped and supported. That is what the church is for. The New Testament knows nothing of the sole Christian, or the one-man evangelist, the lone ranger, setting out valiantly to take on the enemy alone. We are a band of brothers and sisters. We are not alone.

That is why we are to be committed to church-based persuasive evangelism. Engaging with atheists is done through the local body of Christ. In this body each of us is only a part. We are team players. We are not the coach.

Most work of the Spirit is done "in the secret place". It happens under the radar. It is God working imperceptibly through a thousand different threads, weaving his grand design. But that does not mean that we should not prepare, pray, plan and train. The sad thing is that many churches regard evangelism in general as a kind of add-on to the Christian life and to their programmes. Have you ever noticed how much of church life is geared towards maintenance and keeping the saints happy—so that they don't wander off to another church?

But let us say that you are in the blessed position of being part of a local church that believes that evangelism is to be part of its DNA. A church which wants to reach out as a whole to those who are far from God. A church that not only accepts that the good news is to be proclaimed to those within it, but also to those who seem the most difficult and hardened against the good news. How can that church engage with atheists?

Church-based persuasive evangelism is a neat sounding phrase which, when unpacked, gives us a beautiful and biblical picture of how mission can work. The church is the called people of God, seeking to live together in love and harmony, listening to the Lord speaking through his word, talking to the Lord in prayer and experiencing the gifts and blessings of the Holy Spirit.

As the body of Christ, we reflect the heart of Christ for the whole world. We too weep over our own Jerusalem and long for the harvest to be gathered in (Matthew 23 v 37). Evangelism is simply the communication of the good news about Jesus Christ. Evangelism acknowledges that the human race is far worse that we think, and that we are far more loved than we ever imagine we could be. It is good news for broken people. A cure for cancer is not good news for people who don't accept that cancer exists or that they might have it. Only when people realise they are broken people living in a broken world will they seek the "fix" of the gospel. That is why our evangelism has to be "persuasive". We cannot and should not expect people just to believe because we do, or because we say so. We should not seek to brainwash people or emotionally blackmail them. To do so is dishonouring to Christ. Instead we seek to provide people with *reasons* to believe. And the church is the best place to do that.

To some that is counterintuitive. Maybe you have bought into the narrative that Jesus is cool, but the church is a place full of hypocrites that puts people off Christ. Most people who think that Jesus is cool are like Elton John, who stated that Jesus would be for same-sex marriage because he was a "great guy". They have no idea who Jesus is, what he claimed, or what he did. They just like the image—an image created in their own likeness.

And neither do they know the church. Of course there are hypocrites. (I usually try to refrain from suggesting that those who don't come to church because it's "full of hypocrites" are making a mistake because they would fit right in!) But that is what the Bible says—all of us are sinners. I tell people that we are a group of messed-up people in a messed-up world, with a great Saviour. Once people see real Christianity in action it is the most difficult thing to dismiss.

As a young man, I knew all the arguments against Christianity and I often used them. But my mind was blown away by meeting genuine Christians who really believed it and who really tried to live it. They were not mad or deluded, and it looked as though there was something real. This, of course, is the biblical pattern.

> By this everyone will know that you are my disciples, if you love one another. *John 13 v 35*

Would it not be wonderful if people came into our public gatherings to the effect that Paul describes: "So they will fall down and worship God, exclaiming, 'God is really among you!'" (1 Corinthians 14 v 25)? So the church itself is one of the best apologetics for the gospel.

When I do a *Quench* coffee-shop event, I tell the organisers what they need: prayer, good publicity, a decent "neutral" venue, a good chairperson, great coffee and a church where Jesus is. I need to be able to say at the end of an evening's discussion and questions,

> I have tried to remove some of your defeater beliefs, I have tried to show you that belief in Jesus is rational and reasonable. Now if you want to meet Jesus—you see those people?—go to their church, meet with them, and you will meet with Jesus.

That's why the church as the people of God is so vital in engaging with atheists. The bride points to the bridegroom and invites those who say there is no wedding to the ultimate wedding feast.

Contact, connect, communicate

The church is also integral to engaging with atheists in other ways. First, by providing suitable *contact events*. These are a kind of pre-evangelism, seeking to provide a safe and secure environment in order to make contact with those who are outside the church. These may occur within church premises—music concerts, games, lectures, food nights, etc. Or they may be off the premises—five-a-side football, hill walking, community barbecues, etc. They are not overtly evangelistic. You do not have to pray together before you play football, the music does not have to be "Christian" and the food does not need an overtly Christian after-dinner speaker. These things are good for a church to do in and of themselves.

Another way some churches have found helpful for building friendships with local people is to run a book club where current and classic books are read and discussed. Everything from Nick Hornby to Dostoevsky can be suitable. All really great books in classic and modern literature deal with gospel themes. Another possibility is to have a movie discussion group.[11]

More overtly evangelistic events do require specific gospel communication. Having a meal with an after-dinner speaker is a great way to introduce the gospel. Going to a local coffee shop and having a speaker followed by questions and discussion has proved very effective. You could even try holding a debate—where you can assure your atheist friend that both sides will be well represented. Another way is to have a gospel music concert. These

---

11 Damaris Trust provides excellent material to help facilitate discussion about many current films. www.damaris.org.uk

are what we call **connect events**, where we are seeking to connect those who come with the good news.

Finally, there are **communicate events**, where there is opportunity to go into more depth about what Christian teaching is. This can range from a *Christianity Explored* or *Alpha* course to your regular or even special Sunday services. You might also have a Christian book club, or a film night that looks at things from a specifically Christian viewpoint.

Every local church should seek, either on their own or with others, to provide a regular diet of non-cringeworthy events that Christians will feel confident about inviting their non-Christian friends to.

Prayer

The most powerful tool we have in engaging with atheists, however, is prayer. It is good to talk to men and women about God. It is even better to talk to God about men and women.

One lady whose door we knocked on during a particular mission week was very antagonistic—but at the end of the mission, out of the hundreds of people contacted, she was the only one who came to faith in Christ—and years later she is still going strong with the Lord. I noticed that, without instruction, at every prayer meeting her name was mentioned. It seems as though the Lord laid a real burden on our hearts for her.

Imagine if everyone in your church regularly prayed for six non-Christian friends. Of course it is not a matter of mechanics or mathematics, but regular, heartfelt systematic prayer for people is the absolute key. You would pray regularly for your neighbour, workmate, friend or family member if they were diagnosed with terminal cancer. So why not pray for them when they have been diagnosed with a far worse disease—with much more serious consequences? How much must we hate someone not to pray for them?! Our church prayer meetings (you do have a church prayer meeting, don't you?) should not just be an organ recital (*we pray for Mrs Smith's heart, Mr Brown's lungs, Joe Blow's kidneys*), but rather a storming of the gates of hell and a pleading with the throne of heaven to come and save.

Internet and social media

There are of course many fine websites which provide excellent materials on communicating the gospel. For atheists, the evangelistic sermons of Tim Keller are an example of a great resource[12]—my own sister was converted through my son downloading many of them onto her phone. The UCCF website[13] also has excellent resources. And of course I would encourage you to use the material produced by my organisation, Solas[14]. There are many others of varying quality—the best I have listed in the resources section on page 113.

But our churches should learn to use the internet and social media in a much more effective way. Do you have a fresh, clear and regularly updated website, that you would be quite happy to point your atheist friends to? Is

---

12 www.redeemer.com

13 www.bethinking.org

14 www.solas-cpc.org

the website address visible outside your church on posters and billboards? Is it visible on all your church literature? It may even be worth having a small card with the website address on it that you can give to those who will not come to church—through the medium of the internet, church can come to them! Why not film some short video testimonies of members of the congregation and post them on YouTube?

What kind of creative and artistic people do you have in your church, whose gifts could be used in this way?

Many people in your congregation will be on Facebook and Twitter as individuals. While not every post of theirs will be a Bible verse (although that would be a whole lot better than having endless pictures of your food or cats), social media is useful for starting conversations and sharing what is most important to you. It's also a great way to let people know what events are happening in your church.

Apologetics training

> But in your hearts revere Christ as Lord. Always be prepared to give an answer to everyone who asks you to give the reason for the hope that you have. But do this with gentleness and respect.
>
> 1 Peter 3 v 15

This is the key verse for all apologists. And all of us are to be apologists. Sadly, apologetics has bad connotations for many believers. There are those who think that it sounds too much like you're saying sorry for being a Christian.

There are others who, aware that they are not an Oxbridge professor and struggled with science at school, feel that it is not something they're capable of understanding. Plus the whole area of apologetics can have the same "nerdy" feel as computer programming!

But the Latin term *apologia* actually means "defence of". In that all Christians are called to proclaim and defend the good news, we are all apologists. The trouble is that many of us not only *feel* inadequate for the task, we actually *are* inadequate. We need the help of the Holy Spirit and the teaching of the church.

Is your church regularly providing training in persuasive evangelism? Are you taught not only the basics of the word but also how to connect that word to today's culture? Do you discuss the questions that people are asking? This is a vital area for today's church and it should begin from a very young age. Pray and make it a priority for your teenagers, young people and older people.

Persuasive preaching

Which leads us on to the kind of preaching you are being fed with. All good preachers will preach from the Bible. They will do so in a consecutive, expository and Spirit-filled way. And they will also preach in a *contemporary* way. This doesn't mean that they will drive up to the pulpit on a Harley-Davidson, with their ponytail hanging over their leather jacket. It *does* mean that they will do the "double-listening" John Stott spoke of—listening to the word of God in the Scriptures, and listening to the questions and answers of fallen humanity in the world.

Why not encourage your pastor to have one sermon

every now and then that deals with a particular question that your atheist friends are asking? Once that happens you will feel a lot more confident about inviting them.

In a good church, preachers should also be aware that there will be atheists, sceptics and doubters in the congregation. Not so that they can criticise them and blast them with the gospel. But rather so that they will be careful about how they phrase their arguments and encouragements to believers, and will not caricature atheists in an offensive way, or speak dismissively of unbelievers.

There is so much that the church could and should be doing. Equipping, loving, praying, resourcing, training, facilitating, worshipping, fellowship, bible teaching and so much more. All of this provides the context in which you can reach out as a church.

There is an old adage that it takes a church to raise a child. It also takes a church to reach an atheist.

Guillaume's story

I grew up in a wonderfully loving family in France, near Paris. My dad was a mathematician and computer scientist, and my mother "religiously" devoted herself to the well-being and education of her children. All in all, I was pretty happy with my life, and in a thoroughly secular culture.

On holiday, I met a girl from New York, who believed in God—an intellectual suicide by my standards. We started dating, and my new goal in life was to explain to her why all this was untenable, so that she could put this nonsense behind her, and we could be together without her misconceptions standing in the way. So I started thinking about the whole thing. What good reason was there to think God exists, and what good reason was there to think atheism was true instead?

So I picked up a Bible to figure it out. And at the same time, since I'm a scientist, I figured there was at least one experiment that could be carried out to disconfirm the belief that God exists: I thought "if any of this is true, then there is a God who exists right now and presumably cares greatly about this project of mine", so I started to pray with the air as an atheist: "If there is a God, then here I am, I'm looking into this, why don't you go ahead and reveal yourself to me. I'm open." Well, I wasn't, really, but I figured that shouldn't stop God if he existed.

So I read in the Gospels about this Jesus of Nazareth. And there, it didn't exactly feel like what I expected. I was impressed by the authority of that man's teaching. Additionally, even as an atheist, I knew that the person of Jesus of Nazareth was not just a piece of mythology; it seemed clear he was at least a person of history who walked the roads of Palestine in the first century, and apparently his story was compelling enough that these ancient followers of his believed it and even suffered for preaching his death and resurrection. These considerations were making it harder to completely throw out the whole thing, and I knew that at some point I would need to give a coherent account of who I thought Jesus in fact was.

I decided I would try and visit a church, to see what those Christians do when they get together. Frankly, I went to that church like I would go to the zoo: to see some weird exotic animals that I had read about in books, but had never seen in real life. I remember thinking that if any of my friends or family could see me there in church I would die of shame. I also remember finding it troubling to see that these people seemed to actually believe what they practiced. They genuinely thought their prayers were being heard by God.

I don't remember a word that the preacher said on that day. He finished his sermon, and I thought, "I have heard enough, I saw what I needed to see, now let me get out of here". I jumped on my feet, and started quickly walking down the aisle toward the large exit door at the back of the church, very carefully avoiding making eye contact with anybody, so that I wouldn't have to introduce myself to any of these people.

I reached the back door, opened it, and I literally had one foot out the door, when I was suddenly stopped in my tracks, as a strong chilling blast in my chest went up from my stomach all the way to my throat. I stopped there, frozen on the spot with goose bumps all over, and heard myself saying: *"this is ridiculous, I have to figure this out"*.

So I put my foot back in, closed the door in front of me, turned around, and went straight to the head pastor. *"So, you believe in God, ugh?"* —*"Yes"*, he responded with a smile. *"So how does that work out?"* I asked. *"We can talk about it"*, he said. And after people left, we went to his office. He briefly prayed for me, which I obviously felt a bit awkward about, but at least it was reassuringly consistent: he really believed in it. And we started to talk...

*You can read the rest of Guillaume's story at **theologui.blogspot.com***

*You can view a video of his story at **www.cbn.com***

Do get some apologetics training. Although I prefer not to use the 'A' word. Its better to think of it as persuasive evangelism.

Don't just moan about your church's lack of evangelistic zeal. Seek to set an example.

Do connect with other like-minded believers from other churches. If we can't work together in proclaiming the gospel what hope do we have?

Don't waste all your time on internet conversations—get some real "friends" and follow Jesus rather than seeking "followers" for yourself.

Do begin with prayer, personal and corporate. Don't decide to do something and then seek the Lord's blessing. Seek his blessing and guidance first.

Don't fall for the "lie" that your non-Christian friends won't like your church. You don't know. They may be pleasantly surprised, as may you!

Do ensure that your church has a decent supply of resources. A good website, a small but clear book-stall with several of the best evangelistic books, and an open meeting space (with decent coffee) all help.

Don't just leave evangelism to paid "professionals". We are all witnesses called to gossip the gospel.

Do practice hospitality. In every culture that has ever existed throughout the world, the basics of food, family and friends are connect points we all have.

Chapter Seven

Conclusion

St Augustine prayed, "Thou hast made us for thyself, O Lord, and our hearts are restless until they find their rest in thee". If you said to most atheists that they had a "God-shaped hole" in their lives they would understandably be offended. But you don't need to tell them. They do have such a gap. The Verve had a wonderful song which describes contemporary life: *Bittersweet Symphony*. In it the writer describes this ache in his life:

> Well I never pray
> But tonight I'm on my knees yeah
> I need to hear some sounds that recognise the
> pain in me, yeah

When we are seeking to bring Christ to people we should operate on the basis that we are hearing the pain in people and speaking words which bring healing. We seek to bring Christ. You do not counter atheism with theism.

You counter atheism with Christ. No one who meets with the Risen Christ remains an atheist!

Confirming nostalgia

Pasolini, the gay Marxist atheist, made an extraordinary film about Jesus in 1964: *The Gospel according to St. Matthew*. In it he used only the words of the Gospel for dialogue. He was asked at a press conference in 1966 why he as an unbeliever had made such a religious film. His reply was honest and revealing:

> If you know that I am an unbeliever, then you know me better than I do myself. I may be an unbeliever who has a nostalgia for a belief.

Like the Scottish writer who told me that, although he was an atheist, he would describe himself as a *Presbyterian* atheist because, while he believed there was no God, he was always looking over his shoulder to see if he was there! Our job is to confirm atheists' often repressed suspicions and instincts that God is here, that he is incarnate in Christ, and that belief is much much more than nostalgia or wishful thinking.

Of course, we know that people cannot see the kingdom unless, according to Jesus, they are born of the Spirit. Paul says:

> Our gospel came to you not simply with words but also with power, with the Holy Spirit and with deep conviction.   *1 Thessalonians 1 v 5*

That again is why we do the work of engaging with atheists as people utterly dependent on God, knowing that we simply *cannot* do it. But we do so in *confidence* that this is what God has called us to do and that his word will not return to him empty but will accomplish that for which it was sent.

And it does.

There are many people who used to be "religious" but have become atheist. But there are as many, if not more, stories of those who used to be atheists but have become believers. Let me close this short book by telling you of just a few of them that I have known—so that you may be encouraged, and know that your labour in the Lord is not in vain, because he who is for us is greater than the hordes against.

Richard Morgan was a keen member of the Dawkins website and regularly used to participate in the ongoing attacks on yours truly—even writing a piece of music entitled *The Wee Flea!* And then God worked in his life, through a variety of means. We liked his story so much that it is now a chapter in *The Dawkins Letters*. It is a great encouragement that God can even use Dawkins to help bring people to himself!

Alistair McGrath, now a writer and theologian, writes of his experience as an atheist.

It was only when I went up to Oxford in 1971 to study chemistry in detail that I began to realise how little I knew about the history and philosophy of the natural sciences, or the nature of Christian belief. Like my fellow countryman, C. S. Lewis, I found myself experiencing "the steady unrelenting approach of him whom I so earnestly desired not to meet". To cut a long story short, I discovered what I did not really understand, and accepted what I increasingly came to realise was an imaginatively impoverished and emotionally deficient substitute.

Heather Tomlinson was a journalist who was brought to faith in Christ. You can read her testimony of her journey to faith in the book *Why I am not an Atheist*, which was written as a response to Bertrand Russell's *Why I am not a Christian*.

Antony Flew was the Richard Dawkins of his age—the most famous English-speaking atheist in the world. Until Associated Press reported an extraordinary change—so extraordinary that Dawkins and other more militant atheists speculated that he had gone senile!

A British Philosophy professor who has been a leading champion of atheism for more than half a century has changed his mind. He now believes in God more or less based on scientific evidence.

Flew himself says:

In a 1976 debate with Prof Thomas Warren in Texas I stated, "I know there is no God". I have followed the argument where it has led me. And it has led me to accept the existence of a self-existent, immutable, immaterial, omnipotent and omniscient being.

I would highly recommend Flew's last book, *There is a God* (HarperOne, 2007).

I met **P** in a pub in west London just before I was due to speak at an outreach event in a local Baptist church. He had come up from the south especially for the event, and it was one of those wonderful "God-incidences" that we met and were able to chat. Some time later he heard William Lane Craig and as a result came to faith in Christ. Peter's story is an example of how God can use "chance" meetings, as well as intentional ones. Every salvation is a story of a chain with a thousand links. What you do, what you say and what you are can be one of those links for many, many people.

L is a Chinese girl who had never read a Bible and knew nothing about Jesus. She was brought up as an atheist. I met her at a *Christianity Explored* group that we were holding. She was crying. "What's wrong?" I asked. "It's Jesus—he is just so beautiful." Sometimes when we are used to the religious jargon and clichés, we forget just how beautiful Jesus is. It's not our job to make him beautiful, it's our job to tell people about him. How can they believe unless they hear? That's again why I stress how important it is that you have at least one readable book about Jesus ready to give to others.

M was another atheist who came to a *CE* course. "Why are you here?" "Well, I was brought up an atheist, but I'm beginning to have my doubts." I loved it. A backslidden atheist! May there be many more.

And finally, and for me most personally, my sister **Fiona**. A smart, intelligent, compassionate woman who was without Christ and without hope in this world. Through a combination of my son, Tim Keller's sermons and many other parts of a complex jigsaw that is every person's testimony and life, she came to faith, was baptized, married and is now working with her husband (who also became a believer) in a Church in the Scottish Highlands. Never give up on anyone. Your calling is not to determine who goes to heaven; your calling is to point the way.

Why bother?

I sometimes get asked: *Why do you bother? You will never persuade anyone.* I agree. It is not up to me to persuade them. When Paul was asked by King Agrippa if he thought that he could persuade Agrippa to be a Christian, he responded:

> Short time or long—I pray to God that not only you but all who are listening to me today may become what I am, except for these chains. **Acts 26 v 29**

We engage with atheists, not because we want to win an argument, nor because we regard them as a threat, but rather because we love them and want them to know the best life for all. I love the way that Richard Morgan describes his new life in Christ:

> As I considered my perception of life, the universe and everything, it was literally as if I had been looking at a two-dimensional image in black and white, and in an instant everything became three dimensional and technicolour!

May the Lord grant that you and all those with whom you share Christ come to know this glorious, colourful, multi-dimensional eternal life.

Resources

Atheism

There are many books by and about the New Atheists but it is not necessary to read them all.

Alister McGrath's *The Twilight of Atheism* is a helpful overview of the current state of atheism in the modern world.

Richard Dawkins' *The God Delusion* is the basic textbook of the New Fundamentalist Atheists.

Alain de Botton's *Religion for Atheists* takes the softer approach.

Bertrand Russell's collection of essays *Why I am not a Christian* is dated but is the root from which the more modern atheists flow.

Atheist Delusions by David Bentley Hart is a more academic account of how the new atheism is not really new at all.

Christopher Hitchens' *God is Not Great*. Hitchens is the most entertaining and easiest to read of all the New Atheists. Be warned however that his book is badly titled. There is very little about God and a great deal about the misdeeds and errors of the religious.

Michel Onfray's *In Defence of Atheism* is a classic statement of hardcore atheism in the European tradition.

A. C. Grayling's *Against All Gods* is short and bitter.

John Gray is an honest and provocative atheist philosopher. His *Black Mass, Apocalyptic Religion and the Death of Utopia* is a sobering assessment of where utopian atheism leads.

There are numerous atheist websites and blogs which exemplify what I speak about in chapters one and two. In terms of more populist portrayals of atheism and the atheist view of Christianity, most of the western media—from the BBC through to Hollywood and CNN—provides adequate evidence of the current atheist mood in our culture.

Christian approaches

"Of making many books there is no end, and much study wearies the body." (Ecclesiastes 12 v 12b) There are so many good, bad and indifferent books on all the above subjects, it's hard to know where to begin. I would suggest the following as good books to be familiar with yourself and to have to pass on to others. You may of course be aware of others and create your own list.

How Prayer Impacts Lives (CFP) is a valuable book with short testimonies about prayer, useful for believers and non-believers alike.

New Atheism, A Survival Guide, by Graham Veale (CFP), is excellent for understanding where many of the new atheists are coming from.

John Stackhouse's *Humble Apologetics* (OU Press) is a beautifully written and very helpful guide to how we engage.

Why Trust the Bible? by Amy Orr-Ewing (IVP, 2005) is an excellent introduction to some of the main questions that people ask.

Vishnal Mangalwadi's *The Book that made your World* (Thomas Nelson) should be required reading for all! I have never read anything better.

John Lennox's *God's Undertaker* (Lion, 2009) is the book I always recommend on the science/faith dialogue.

Is God a Moral Monster (Baker 2011) by Paul Copan is the best book I have read on the vexed question of the God of the Old Testament.

And for the current shibboleth question of our culture, Sam Allberry's *Is God Anti-Gay?* (Good Book Company, 2013), is essential.

Anything by C. S. Lewis is worth reading; his *Mere Christianity* is still one of the most thought provoking introductions to Christianity for the "common" man.

The modern C.S. Lewis is Tim Keller and his *Reason for God* (Hodder and Stoughton) is the best contemporary book to give to the thinking literate person.

It is essential to have a book explaining who Christ is. I really couldn't find one so I wrote *Magnificent Obsession* (CFP). Whether you use that, or similar, it is essential that you have something which gives people the story about Jesus.

I wrote *The Dawkins Letters* (CFP) as an attempt to engage with the New Atheism. There are many other excellent responses.

The Bible

The New Bible Commentary is an invaluable tool for all bible study.

What the Bible Means to Me (CFP) is a good book to give to people as a testimony about how the Bible works in people's lives.

When studying any particular book of the Bible, there are many excellent commentaries. Unless you actually want to study Greek and Hebrew, avoid the more technical ones and stick to well-written, contemporary, faithful books such as *The Bible Speaks Today series* (IVP), or the more recent study guides *God's Word for You* (The Good Book Company).

There are a wealth of bible study resources (and sermons) by Tim Keller on the Redeemer Church website (www.redeemer.com)

Tolle, Lege... Take and read!

Church-based evangelism

Outgrowing the Ingrown Church (Zondervan 1986), by C. John Miller is a challenging read and will help you to think about what kind of church you are.

Greg Koukl's *Tactics* (Zondervan, 2009) is suggestive and helpful, as is *Questioning Evangelism* by Randy Newman.

If you are interested in coffee-shop evangelism then read *Quench, Coffee Shop Evangelism* (available from Solas CPC).

Websites

There are many websites that offer very helpful material.

Ravi Zacharias has some great resources:

www.rzim.org

www.bethinking.org is my favourite go-to site for students.

www.euroleadership.org has some great webinars and teaching videos on numerous subjects.

www.solas-cpc.org has debates, papers, videos, etc. on all the above subjects.

There is some excellent training material at the *Stand to Reason* website: **www.str.org**

And finally, the *Christianity Explored* website features outline answers to a lot of apologetic questions, as well as featuring some video testimonies and links to local churches where people can join a discussion course.

www.christianityexplored.org

uestions
Christians ask

An excellent series for building your own faith, and helping others discover the Christian message for themselves

Is God anti-Gay?
by Sam Allberry

Christians, the church and the Bible seem to be out of step with modern attitudes toward homosexuality.

In this short, simple book, Sam Allberry wants to help confused Christians understand what God has said about these questions in the Scriptures, and offers a positive and liberating way forward through the debate.

Can I really trust the Bible?
by Barry Cooper

The Bible makes big claims for itself. But do those claims stand up? Aren't the stories just legends? Hasn't the information been corrupted over time? Isn't the Bible full of mistakes? And isn't it culturally outdated?

In this absorbing little book, Barry Cooper explores these questions —and many others— with warmth, wit and integrity.

Order from your local Good Book website:
UK & Europe: www.thegoodbook.co.uk
North America: www.thegoodbook.com
Australia: www.thegoodbook.com.au
New Zealand: www.thegoodbook.co.nz

An excellent series for building your own faith, and helping others discover the Christian message for themselves

How can I be sure?
by John Stevens

Many Christians experience times of doubt and uncertainty. At various times we can ask: Does God love me? Am I really a Christian?—and even—Is there a God at all?!

This short, readable book unpacks the difference between good and bad doubt, shows us where it comes from and how to deal with it in ourselves and others. It explains clearly and simply the liberating reality of what the Bible tells us about doubt, assurance and the Christian life.

What happens when I die?
by Marcus Nodder

We all have questions about death. Despite the strong assurance the Bible gives us about life beyond the grave, Christians are often troubled by other questions. What will happen on the day of judgement? Will we have bodies in heaven? Will there be rewards?

These short, simple books are designed to help Christians understand what God has said about these questions in the scriptures.

Other titles in this series

Engaging with Hindus
by Robin Thomson

Hindus are the third largest faith in the world, and yet many Christians know very little about their beliefs and lifestyle

This short book is designed to help both Christians and whole churches understand more about Hindus, and to reach out to them with the good news of the Gospel.

Robin Thomson spent twenty years in India teaching the Bible and training church leaders. He is the author of several books relating the Bible to Asian culture

Engaging with Muslims
by John Klaassen

Many Christians in the west are fearful of engaging in conversation with Muslims—believing that they will be hostile to Christian beliefs and conversations about the Bible.

This short book is designed to help both Christians and whole churches understand more about the variety of Muslims there are living in the west, and to reach out to them with the good news of the Gospel.

John Klaassen is Associate Professor of Christian Missions at Boyce College, in Louisville, USA. Previously he worked in relief, development and mission work in North Africa. He is married to Shari and has two children.

Order from your local Good Book website:
UK & Europe: www.thegoodbook.co.uk
North America: www.thegoodbook.com
Australia: www.thegoodbook.com.au
New Zealand: www.thegoodbook.co.nz

thegoodbook
COMPANY
Opening up the Bible

At The Good Book Company, we are dedicated to helping Christians and local churches grow. We believe that God's growth process always starts with hearing clearly what He has said to us through His timeless word—the Bible.

Ever since we opened our doors in 1991, we have been striving to produce resources that honor God in the way the Bible is used. We have grown to become an international provider of user-friendly resources to the Christian community, with believers of all backgrounds and denominations using our Bible studies, books, evangelistic resources, DVD-based courses and training events.

We want to equip ordinary Christians to live for Christ day by day, and churches to grow in their knowledge of God, their love for one another, and the effectiveness of their outreach.

Call us for a discussion of your needs or visit one of our local websites for more information on the resources and services we provide.

UK & Europe: www.thegoodbook.co.uk
North America: www.thegoodbook.com
Australia: www.thegoodbook.com.au
New Zealand: www.thegoodbook.co.nz

UK & Europe: 0333 123 0880
North America: 866 244 2165
Australia: (02) 6100 4211
New Zealand (+64) 3 343 1990

www.christianityexplored.org

Our partner site is a great place for those exploring the Christian faith, with a clear explanation of the good news, powerful testimonies and answers to difficult questions.

One life! What's it all about?